Pembroke College, Cambridge

The Buildings and Gardens

Pembroke College, Cambridge

The Buildings and Gardens

Edited by
Chris Smith

This edition © Scala Arts and Heritage, 2025
Text and illustrations © Pembroke College, Cambridge 2025

First published in 2025 by
Scala Arts & Heritage Publishers Ltd
43 Great Ormond Street
London WC1N 3HZ
www.scalapublishers.com
An imprint of B. T. Batsford Holdings Ltd.

In association with
Pembroke College
Trumpington Street
Cambridge CB2 1RF

Hardback ISBN 978-1-78551-533-0
Paperback ISBN 978-1-78551-534-7

Managing Editor, Scala: Claire Young
Project Editor: Catherine Bradley
Designer: Matthew Wilson / Mexington.co.uk
Printed in Turkey

All rights reserved. No part of this book may be reproduced, stored in a retrieval system or transmitted in any form or by any means electronic, mechanical, photocopying, recording or otherwise, without the written permission of Pembroke College, Cambridge and Scala Arts & Heritage Publishers Ltd.

Every effort has been made to acknowledge correct copyright of images where applicable. Any errors or omissions are unintentional and should be notified to the Publisher, who will arrange for corrections to appear in any reprints.

Front cover *Library Lawn at Pembroke, with Christopher Wren's 1665 Chapel behind.*

Back cover *Library Lawn at Pembroke, seventeenth-century chimneys and the College gardens beyond.*

Inside front cover *Pembroke's new Mill Lane development, fronting on to Trumpington Street, with the new Gatehouse in the middle and the Auditorium (the former United Reformed Church) on the left.*

Inside back cover *The former Trumpington Street frontage of what has now become Pembroke's new Mill Lane development.*

Frontispiece *The view from Red Buildings Lawn towards the Library and Library Lawn.*

Contents

Introduction — 6

Part I: Evolving Architecture
1. Pembroke College: An Architectural Tour — 14
2. The Architecture of Mill Lane — 30
3. Acquiring the Mill Lane Site — 42

Part II: Ray Dolby and his Legacy
4. Ray Dolby at Cambridge — 50
5. The History of the Mill Lane Site — 54
6. The Mill Lane Gardens — 64
7. The Environmental Sustainability of the Mill Lane Site — 68

Part III: Study and Reflection
8. Pembroke's Gardens — 78
9. The Old Library — 88
10. Ridley's Walk: A Protestant Martyr, an Orchard, a Banana and Two Inventors — 98
11. The Library at Pembroke — 106
12. The Cloisters — 116

Part IV: Art and Life
13. The Art of Pembroke — 126
14. Room N8B — 138
15. The Pembroke Smoking Concert — 144
16. Pembroke Today: The Buildings We Made Our Own — 150

Timeline — *156*
Acknowledgements — *158*

Introduction

Chris Smith

RAY DOLBY CAME TO PEMBROKE IN 1957 AS A Marshall Scholar to study for a PhD in X-ray microscopy. He went on to become a Research Fellow, but soon afterwards he found a way to eliminate the hiss on sound recordings, a discovery that revolutionised listening for the world. Dolby Sound is now embedded in virtually everything we see and hear. When he left his bequest in 2013 for 'the buildings and grounds of Pembroke College', it was the largest single gift then ever given to an Oxford or Cambridge College. We were determined to make the best possible use of this transformational donation.

For many years we had been hoping to develop the land and buildings along the south side of Mill Lane, directly opposite the Porters' Lodge of our historic College and right beside the precise spot where the medieval heart of the very first Pembroke buildings stood. Now, with Ray Dolby's generous bequest, the possibility became real, enabling us to embark on the creation of a wholly new part of Pembroke. We had to raise substantial

Lord Chris Smith, Master of Pembroke, in Pembroke's Library.

Opposite *Old Court at night. Dating from the late fourteenth century, this is the oldest part of any Cambridge College still in daily use.*

The historic frontage of Pembroke, harmoniously combining the medieval entrance from 1389 and Sir Christopher Wren's Chapel from 1665.

New Court, 1881–2, by George Gilbert Scott Jr.

further funds, of course, but the opportunity was now very much there. We seized it.

On this new site beside Mill Lane we have created three new courtyards, a hundred new student rooms, a cluster of teaching, meeting and seminar rooms, an Auditorium, a new Gateway, an exhibition gallery, a social centre with a new café and a range of College and Fellows' offices. I have to confess that my favourite part of the new site is in the tower of the old United Reformed Church (where we have converted the body of the church into the new Auditorium): within the tower, which is hollow inside, we are building a climbing wall. We have also maintained a very important characteristic of historic Pembroke in planning for the new site. In Pembroke there are no completely enclosed courtyards. Every space flows through to a space beyond, usually framed by grass, flower borders and trees. The same is true on the Mill Lane site.

This book celebrates the completion of our new development. It tells the story of the Mill Lane site – its original uses and history, the process of acquisition and of securing planning consent, and the architectural and landscape thinking that went into its conception. It heralds the focus we and our architects have placed on the environmental sustainability of the site. But

Opposite *Stained-glass windows in the College Library by Gottfried von Stockhausen, from 2001, based on drawings by Pembroke naturalists William Turner and Nehemiah Grew.*

Right *Frost on Library Lawn, with Alfred Waterhouse's Library, 1878, on the right and seventeenth-century chimneys on the left.*

Overleaf *The historic frontage of Pembroke from Trumpington Street, from the Porters' Lodge on the left to Red Buildings on the right.*

it also turns its attention to the historic site of Pembroke, exploring how our College has grown organically through the centuries – from the fourteenth century (we have the oldest buildings still in use in any Cambridge College), through the building of our glorious Chapel by the young Christopher Wren, through the dramatic changes wrought by Alfred Waterhouse (and some that were happily prevented) and up to the present day. It looks at some of the specific parts of the historic campus, at individual buildings and rooms, paths, gardens and works of art, along with some of the people through history who have been associated with these. It tells something of the story of Pembroke itself, which will be wonderfully taken forward in the enhanced College we now possess.

When I came up as a student to study English at Pembroke in 1969 I was full of excitement and trepidation, anxiety and awe – and probably a significant dose of imposter syndrome. Coming back as Master, after all these years, has been the honour of my life. Now we have managed to transform the educational opportunities we will be able to offer future generations of students. It has been the most significant change and development in our 677 years of history; and Pembroke can now embrace the future with confidence and ambition.

We entitled our campaign to raise funds for Mill Lane 'The Time and the Place', because this was about seizing the moment and enhancing the place. The title also carries echoes of T S Eliot who wrote, in *Ash Wednesday* (1930):

> Because I know that time is always time
> And place is always and only place
> And what is actual is actual only for one time
> And only for one place
> I rejoice that things are as they are…

INTRODUCTION 11

Part I
Evolving Architecture

1 Pembroke College: An Architectural Tour

Stephen Gage

SEEN FROM TRUMPINGTON STREET, PEMBROKE College presents a varied but comparatively humble architectural display. Moving from the nineteenth to the seventeenth to the fourteenth centuries, its facades reveal the primary architectural epochs of the College with clarity. Alfred Waterhouse's strident Red Buildings contrast with but do not overwhelm Sir Christopher Wren's sedate classical Chapel, its cream-coloured stone blending into the ashlar-faced walls of Hitcham's Cloister and the medieval Porters' Lodge. The College entrance is marked not by a soaring gate tower, but a simple double oriel window that predates the Tudor pomp of later foundations. Yet on entering and emerging through the low entrance passage, a new atmosphere is sensed – a realm of interconnected garden courts that invite discovery, a continually unfolding sense of something just beyond, be it a grand vista or an unexpected corner. More than any individual building, it is this character that makes Pembroke memorable.

Left *Alfred Waterhouse by Sir Lawrence Alma-Tadema, oil on canvas, 1891. Waterhouse was Pembroke's principal architect in the 1870s.*

Old Court from the Porters' Lodge c.1870–2, before Waterhouse removed the right-hand range in 1874.

Many other Cambridge Colleges reveal the slow accretion and changing tastes of centuries, but few match Pembroke's blending of architecture and setting, of intimacy alongside scenic variety. Existing accounts have presented chronological rundowns, minute historical facts and curious details, but it is this unique spatial character that I wish to trace in this introduction to Pembroke's architecture. While this quality has been almost entirely absent from historical accounts, it lies at the heart of all who experience the College, whether for a fleeting visit or on a daily basis.

In this story of Pembroke's architecture, one architect looms larger than any other. Not the illustrious Wren, but that great Victorian 'vandal' Alfred Waterhouse. His dramatic expansion of Pembroke in the 1870s helped to create the atmosphere we appreciate today, and yet his work is still usually treated with scepticism, if not gleeful disdain. As the great architectural historian Nikolaus Pevsner characteristically complained in *The Buildings of England: Cambridgeshire* (1954),

In every case where [Waterhouse] added at Pembroke, he spoiled something that was there and replaced by something out of keeping with Cambridge.

It is true that if Waterhouse had his way, there would be almost nothing left of the original College. But if everything ancient had been kept, would Pembroke be a better place today? I would argue most definitively no. It is rather the imperfect but engaging combination of Waterhouse's grand ambitions and Pembroke's humble original buildings that have defined the spatial character that we enjoy and celebrate. What follows is a walking tour through the open courts of the College, exploring this unique history of transformation.

OLD COURT

The difficult and at times dramatic collisions which forged Victorian Pembroke are most apparent entering Old Court from the Porters'

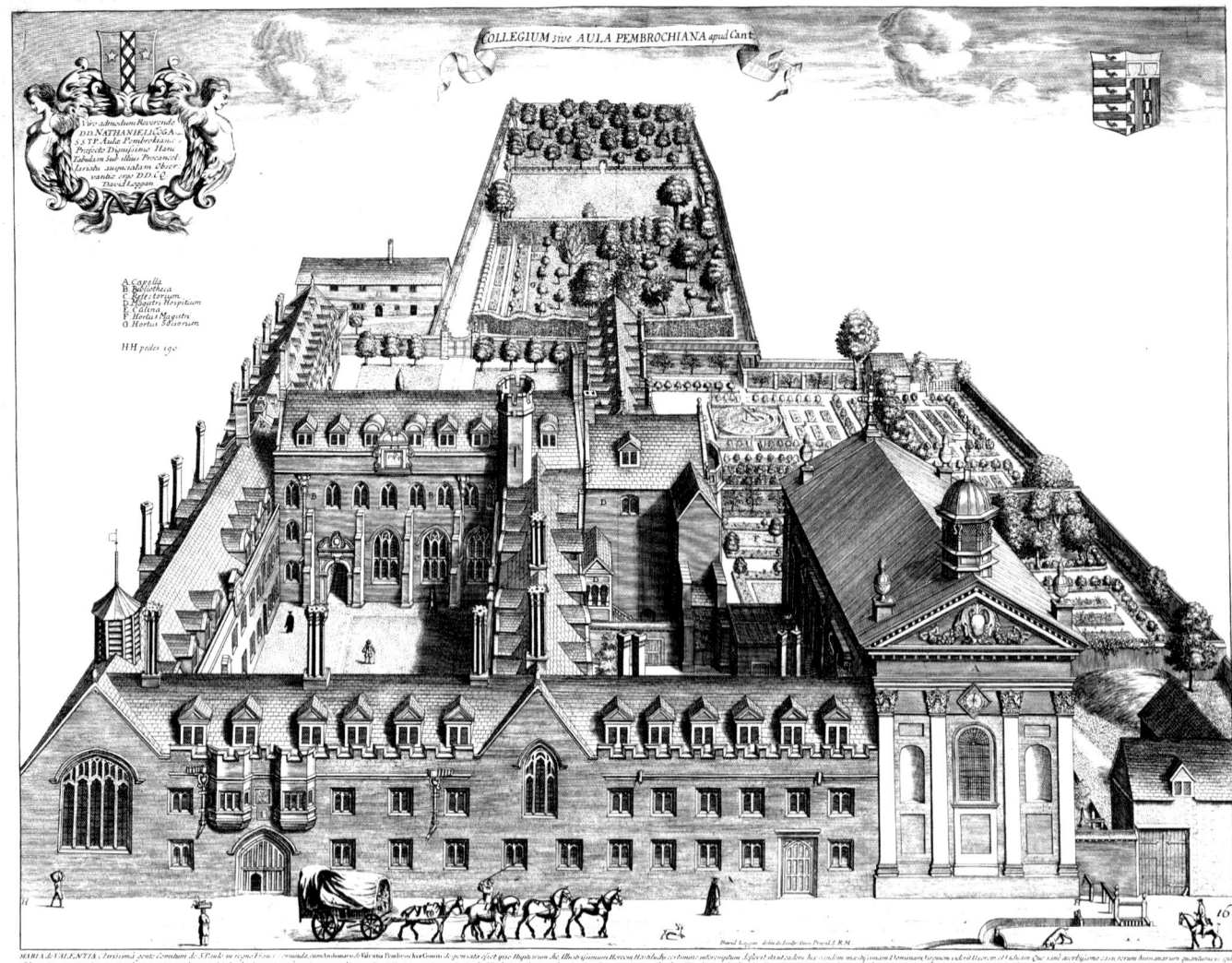

Lodge. A spacious and splendid view immediately unfolds, revealing all principal symbolic buildings of the College. Straight ahead is the Dining Hall (1877), rebuilt by Waterhouse but much changed since. To the right is Wren's stately Chapel (1665), the first truly classical building in Cambridge, subtly extended one bay by George Gilbert Scott Jr in 1882. Situated dramatically between them in the distance is Waterhouse's Library (1878), with its Gothic clocktower of French and Flemish inspiration. It is the quintessential Pembroke view, a picturesque assemblage that Waterhouse

David Loggan's engraving of Pembroke. Loggan published a range of bird's-eye-view engravings, first of Oxford Colleges and then those of Cambridge. The latter appeared in Cantabrigia Illustrata, *1690, from which this is taken.*

A drawing of the Trumpington Street frontage of Pembroke in 1794, drawn by J.M.W. Turner at the age of 19.

himself published as the illustrated summary of his work. It is also highly unusual when seen from the standpoint of collegiate architecture – the traditional collegiate courtyard is enclosed on four sides, with openings strictly controlled through passageways. In Old Court the entire corner is left open, the space of the court blending into adjacent lawns and gardens that surround the library (see pp. 20–1). For this unconventional treatment to be our opening view makes it even more daring, especially for a College founded in 1347.

Yet for most of this long history, a very different view welcomed members – an enclosed court only 52 feet (15.8 metres) wide, less than half its current size. Very few records remain from the medieval period, with no firm building dates, but it is likely that difficulties encountered during the Foundress's initial land purchases accounted for this diminutive size, amongst the smallest in Oxford or Cambridge. Though small, Pembroke's was nevertheless one of the earliest complete examples of the typical collegiate courtyard. David Loggan's famed bird's-eye view of 1690 (p. 16) and photographs taken before Waterhouse's demolitions still give a sense of the original. It can be imagined today by extending a building out across Old Court from the pointed gable end just south of the Porters' Lodge.

Only the (much restored) north and northwest sides of Old Court remain of the original fourteenth-century works, and even these show a history of continual adaptation. The current Old Library was the original chapel, one of the earliest purpose-built collegiate chapels, granted through papal licence. The first Library was added above the Dining Hall in 1452. When Wren's Chapel was completed, the old chapel was converted into a library (1690) with its wonderful woodwork and plastered ceiling. Waterhouse's new Library made this obsolete in turn. After Waterhouse was replaced by Scott Jr, the College Fellows still intended to destroy this magnificent space, carving it up into additional student rooms. Only through judicious delay on Scott's part was it saved, the Fellows finally deciding to keep it as a lecture space.

Looking across the court to Wren's first building, designed as the Sheldonian Theatre in Oxford was also taking shape, we must imagine it as the focus of its own small Chapel Court. This was connected to Old Court via Hitcham's Cloister (now known as the Cloisters), built contemporaneously with the Chapel (originally open underneath for the whole width). Also facing this court was the original Master's Lodge, a ramshackle accretion of spaces including a characteristic Georgian temple front added in 1745. Along with the South Range, this was all demolished in 1874 to make way for the enlarged Hall and Waterhouse's supreme entry view.

WATERHOUSE'S 1870 PLAN

The dramatic opening up of Old Court was part of Waterhouse's comprehensive plan for the College, put forward when he was hired in 1870 by the new Master, John Power. Outlined in a nine-page manuscript letter and accompanying plan drawing, these fascinating documents envisioned even larger changes, including the demolition of Wren's Chapel and the entire front of the College along Trumpington Street.

Opposite *The southern side of Ivy Court, built in 1661. William Pitt lived in the rooms on the first floor when he came to study at Pembroke, aged only 14.*

Below *The Dining Hall, photographed after renovations by John Cory in 1862, before Waterhouse constructed the new Dining Hall in 1875–6.*

Old Court, looking through to Waterhouse's Library, 1878. At Pembroke there are no completely enclosed courtyards, instead always a vista through to something beyond.

This may sound unthinkable today, but in the 1870s the preservation movement was still in its infancy. Furthermore, it was a time of rapid change in educational policy with internal and government-imposed reforms that radically changed the Oxbridge system of education. Such reforms included competitive Honours examinations, new subject areas (especially in the sciences), colleges for women and a greater professionalisation of teaching. It also meant new buildings, dedicated to the larger University. Pembroke's Fellows were intensely worried their large building fund, begun in the eighteenth century to commemorate the poet Thomas Gray, might be appropriated by the larger University. The College was also going through its own rapid expansion, with existing facilities no longer able to accommodate the entire community.

Waterhouse's dramatic plan was thus commensurate with the Master and Fellows' own ambitions. To their vision of a grander College, he added his own architectural skill in planning and picturesque arrangement, fresh from his national competition win for Manchester Town Hall. In addition to two new courts, a redesigned Fellows' Garden and detached Master's Lodge, he proposed a new Chapel. This would be separated from Trumpington Street by a cloister walk to ensure quiet, with a Campanile to provide visual focus to the surrounding courts and gardens. The Campanile would also have augmented the Cambridge skyline and given visual distinction to Pembroke's growing status. As Waterhouse claimed a letter to the Fellows of Pembroke (1870),

> It might be made sufficiently high to be the most conspicuous tower in Cambridge, which suffers much from the lack of lofty architectural features.

THE DINING HALL

In the 1870 plan, the original Dining Hall was retained and extended. However, subsequent studies called into question its structural stability, though its distinctly dilapidated visual appearance probably held greater sway. By early 1875 the Fellows decided to follow Waterhouse's new advice and proceed with demolition. The event remains notorious to this day. It drew the attention of the national press and resulted in a spirited war of letters between old members wishing to save it and those in favour of a new and more impressive structure, including Power and Waterhouse himself. The controversy started in March 1875 with a letter to *The Times*, written by a group of distinguished former members of the College. They deplored the decision for demolition, noting that

> the Hall, erected about 1360, is probably the earliest existing collegiate building of the University, the loss of which, as an example of its age, would be irreplaceable.

Like many Cambridge buildings, the Dining Hall had been altered and partially rebuilt many times through the centuries. The addition of a library above has already been mentioned; when this moved in the seventeenth century, the space over the Dining Hall was converted into rooms. The Hall itself was also remodelled at this time in a Renaissance style with new interior finishes and a new stone entrance (now used as the gate on the far end of Ivy Court). In the 1860s the architect John Cory, a Pembroke alumnus, 'restored' the Dining Hall with more Gothic influences alongside a modern tile floor, gas lighting and new cellars and kitchens. As Waterhouse testily

wrote in defence of his plans, he wanted to clarify the 'real date of the Hall'. To the eyes of an architectural expert, it had little remaining of its authentic medieval appearance apart from the structural make-up of the walls. To members, however, it was a space alive with memory. Edmund Venables, one of the authors of the original complaint, rebutted in a further letter:

> Are we to be blamed if we prefer our 'old lamp' which has called forth so many potent spirits, whose names are our glory, to a 'new lamp', however bright and burnished, but devoid of a single tradition?

Cory argued in similar terms:

> Here the martyr Ridley, the poet Spenser, the statesman Pitt were wont to dine and sup within these very walls.

Their campaign was to no avail, however. Waterhouse proceeded to build his new and much larger Hall, originally with an open timbered roof and stained-glass windows. It gave the College a central communal space commensurate with its growing size and reputation; by the late 1870s it had more than tripled in size from ten years earlier, with over a hundred undergraduate students. Sticking to their decision, the Master and Fellows appear to have been more concerned with the overall planning of the College than any one individual building. The archives contain a very illuminating set of letters written by senior Fellow C.O. Budd, giving insight into the Fellows' intentions and their working relationship with Waterhouse. Initially Waterhouse had proposed building a library on top of the new building, thus recreating its medieval arrangement. His suggestion was vetoed by Budd, who argued that

> less height would be advantageous, as less shutting ... light & air from the inner court, and better harmonising with our other buildings.

Budd went on to propose a freestanding library, as was built shortly after. He and many of the Fellows were clearly supportive of Waterhouse's vision of a modernised College. As Pembroke's constricted medieval layout did not coincide with this vision, it was easily jettisoned.

What the Fellows did come to object to, however, was Waterhouse's forceful architectural style – an eclectic High Victorian Gothic that took free inspiration from numerous sources, including many Continental influences. Budd recorded many visits to Waterhouse's office, asking him to change the Dining Hall elevations,

> to render the façade calmer and more dignified in an architectural sense, by sacrificing some of the extra ornamentation and broken lines ... I felt sure that in doing so I was only expressing what would be the wish of at any rate a majority of our body.

Compared to Red Buildings or the Library, the Dining Hall is certainly tamer, but it still fell out of favour very quickly. In 1926 Maurice Webb removed the open-timbered ceiling to construct two floors of rooms above, thus belatedly reinstating the final configuration of the demolished Dining Hall. In 1949 Murray Easton removed the stained glass in his own restorations. Thus, by degrees, Waterhouse's controversial Gothic Revival showpiece was stripped back and simplified, a closer echo of its demolished forebear.

Ivy Court, with seventeenth-century ranges on either side and the 1875 Dining Hall ahead. Nigel Hall's sculpture, Natural Pearl *(2017) sits in the centre.*

IVY COURT AND RIDLEY'S WALK

Moving through the screens passage into Ivy Court we leave Waterhouse behind, finding ourselves instead in a seventeenth-century three-sided court. The fashion was started by John Caius in the sixteenth century to allow more fresh air, an innovation to the traditional four-sided court that passed Oxford by but flourished at Cambridge. To the left is the North Range, built in 1616 and extended in 1670. To the right is the Hitcham Building of 1661. Both are in a simple domestic style of the period, with few embellishments. The one exception is the curious Renaissance composition on the end of the Hitcham Building near the Dining Hall, probably related to rooms associated with the Master. Today the purity of the court is somewhat interrupted by the Pitt Building (W.D. Caröe,

1 PEMBROKE COLLEGE: AN ARCHITECTURAL TOUR

1907), which creates a greater sense of enclosure on the open end. However, the path leading to a central gate to the Orchard beyond still maintains the original configuration, as seen in Loggan's print (p. 16), while the reuse of the old Dining Hall entrance adds a further touch of the period.

As we pass through the gate, we temporarily leave the courts as the space constricts to a linear path, hemmed in by buildings and heavy planting. Today this beautiful walk enhances the spatial variety, but this was all once part of the Fellows' Garden, and thus restricted to undergraduate students. To get around the problem, Caröe built the gate/upper bridge along Pembroke Street to allow students to reach New Court from the Pitt Building (prior to that, students needed to exit the College and enter again!). Continuing on the path, the Pitt Building gives way to Waterhouse's Master's Lodge (1873), now the Junior Parlour. Originally this was a luxurious freestanding mansion with its own private gardens and carriage entrance along Pembroke Street.

NEW COURT

The contrast between the Victorian red brick of Waterhouse and the golden stone of New Court beyond is immediate. Separated by only ten years, we are in a new architectural era, moving from Waterhouse to Scott Jr, from bold eclecticism to studied restraint and a newfound appreciation of Cambridge precedents, with France and Flanders left far behind. New Court is the direct result of Waterhouse's removal as the College's architect in 1878, just as the Library was being completed. The story is worth telling in detail.

The Master and Fellows met on 30 March 1878 to decide the future development of the College. A wonderful informal note survives which records the detailed votes on these momentous decisions. First, the medieval front of the College, next in line for demolition, was saved in a vote of seven against three. Further, the Chapel was to be extended (not demolished, as recommended by Waterhouse) and the fate of the Old Library consulted on. It was decided the architect for these renovations would not be Waterhouse (five against two, with three abstentions), but the Fellows deferred the choice of a new one.

At the same time they considered building a new block of student rooms. By seven votes to five, it was agreed this was to be a *detached* building on a new site, a (narrow) vote of confidence in Waterhouse's more open planning. Finally, a 'bracket competition' of different architects was set up for the new building's architect. Curiously

Left *The archway from Ivy Court to the Orchard, originally the entrance gateway to the Dining Hall.*

New Court, built by George Gilbert Scott Jr in 1881–2. In summer students play croquet on the lawn.

Waterhouse was still in the mix, alongside the most noted practitioners of the day: George Gilbert Scott, G.F. Bodley, Richard Norman Shaw, Basil Champneys and Reginald Blomfield, as well as the College's previous architect, John Cory. In the final round it came down to Scott and Shaw. Scott was over-whelmingly chosen, 11 against one. In putting Scott's name on the list, the Fellows undoubtedly had in mind the elder Scott, designer of the new chapel for St John's College, St Pancras Station and many other notable works. In an interesting twist of fate, however, he had died three days previously on 27 March. The task therefore fell to his son, George Gilbert Scott Jr.

Sandwiched in between a notable dynasty (his own son, Giles Gilbert Scott, was to be the designer of Battersea Power Station and the iconic red telephone boxes), Scott Jr had a sadder history, being committed to an asylum in 1883 for mental instability. Yet he was an excellent architect and New Court, completed in 1882, is undoubtedly one of Pembroke's finest buildings. Attracting enthusiastic praise since it was first completed, Gavin Stamp summarised it as Scott's 'most admired and influential secular work'. Scott himself described how his designs

> followed the best traditions of Cambridge, with a special reference, too, to the character of the old buildings of Pembroke. I have aimed at a grave academical character, reticent and reserved rather than sensational, and without any exuberance of architectural detail.

While the reference to old Pembroke is a stretch, the building having more affinity with Clare College Old Court or the Fellows' Building at Christ's, this pronounced shift can be seen as a direct response to Budd's pleas for 'harmony' and 'dignity'. After the disruptions of Waterhouse, it was a return to *Cambridge* traditions.

And yet, just as importantly, it carried on Waterhouse's less obvious but vital legacy: the construction of a more open system of garden courts. Scott's L-shaped building formed a loose three-sided court with Waterhouse's Master's Lodge. It framed a landscaped garden lawn that was visually open to the Fellows' Garden beyond, thus creating sweeping green views through the College from its windows. The close vote of the Fellows suggests that departures from the traditional courtyard layout were indeed still controversial. The garden strategy prevailed, however, now executed by Scott in an architectural style that evoked a stronger sense of historical rootedness. New Court was sympathetically extended by Caroe in 1907 along with the new bridge, though in the process it lost some of its original openness.

THE BOWLING GREEN AND ORCHARD

New Court looks across into the Bowling Green and adjoining Orchard. These are among the largest and oldest open spaces of the College. Part of the initial land purchases by the Foundress in the fourteenth century, they were originally walled and separated by a public lane from the main site (the lane was closed in 1620). These are now shielded from the street by Marshall Sisson's Orchard Building (1957) – one of the last 'traditional' buildings in Cambridge, built while Modernism was triumphing at other colleges. Compared to the refinement of New Court, the building's stripped-back Georgian style is slightly incongruous but unobtrusive. It carries on the open-space legacy of its predecessors, putting focus on the careful landscaping and connected pathways of the Bowling Green and Orchard.

FELLOWS GARDEN AND FOUNDRESS COURT

The land now comprising Foundress Court was mostly purchased over the nineteenth century to enlarge the College site. It was united with the older Bowling Green and Orchard to form the picturesque Fellows' Garden in Waterhouse's 1870 plan. Gardens had been vital to colleges since the medieval period, but traditionally they were walled off into discrete entities. As Waterhouse reimagined Pembroke's layout, he began to blur this distinction, the open spaces of the College increasingly unified into a contiguous network. Thus, even though the space was still reserved for Fellows, he made sure to link it visually

Seventeenth-century Ivy Court buildings from the gardens; the chimneys are one of the glories of Pembroke's architecture.

with the surrounding buildings and courts, and preferred landscaping or open gates to walls. In 1933 a new freestanding Master's Lodge was built by Maurice Webb in a simple Georgian style. This existed until the completion of Foundress Court and the rebuilt Lodge, completed by Eric Parry in 1997 as the first substantial new building for the College in 40 years. Foundress Court is an sensitive addition. Similar to New Court a century before, it provides for modern conveniences while fitting comfortably within Pembroke traditions. Though larger and wider, the L-shaped form of the building draws on New Court in the way that it defines the surrounding open space. In attaching the Lodge directly to the building, it harkens back to medieval roots, bypassing the freestanding mansions of Waterhouse and Webb. Foundress Court also cleverly introduces internal garden courtyards to help break up the mass, bringing glimpses of nature and natural light within the internal corridors.

THE LIBRARY LAWN AND RED BUILDINGS LAWN

Passing down the Avenue and through the open gates which once restricted access to the gardens, we come to the Library Lawn, with Red Buildings

Red Buildings from Trumpington Street, built by Alfred Waterhouse in 1872. A French château was the inspiration for Waterhouse's design.

(1872) and their Lawn visible beyond. These spaces adhere closely to Waterhouse's 1870 plan. Though he designated these the 'Third' and 'Fourth' courts, they are really a hybrid between traditional court and garden; the scale is similar to traditional enclosed courts, but the garden planting and moments of open connection create intimacy and informality, even with the grander note of the Library tower.

Such an approach was very new in the 1870s, and there are interesting parallels in other unconventional collegiate work of the period, including William Butterfield's more open quadrangle layout at Keble in Oxford (1868–86) and Basil Champneys' slowly evolving work at Newnham (1875–1910). This careful calibration between architecture and landscape is a hallmark of Waterhouse's achievement and one of the key themes maintained in Pembroke's twentieth-century additions. Even so, the strong presence of Wren's Chapel and the highly picturesque back of the Hitcham Building are still reminiscent of earlier eras.

The space in front of the Library was known as the Undergraduates' Garden. Waterhouse carefully considered the landscaping, noting how he wanted to create a sense of privacy from within the garden, but also to maintain open views between Fellows' Garden and Old Court. The Library itself was innovative in providing lecture and study spaces for undergraduate students, and the great attention Waterhouse gave to these exemplifies the increasing importance of undergraduate life, a key result of the era's reforms.

Old Court: The Cloisters and the Porters' Lodge. From the prominent gable rightwards the buildings are fourteenth century; the cloister dates from the seventeenth century.

BACK TO OLD COURT

Heading to Wren's Chapel at the junction of the courts, we move imperceptibly back into Old Court, completing our circuit of the College. As we have seen, the combination of medieval core and Victorian reinvention has provided controversy and success in equal measure, a situation not paralleled on the same scale by other Colleges. Most kept more remnants of the past. Others, such as Newnham and Selwyn, were built from scratch in a new age, setting a precedent for the more radical Modernist Colleges of the twentieth century, for example Churchill and Robinson.

In closing, it is important to note that the greater openness and new spatial arrangements of Pembroke in the nineteenth century did not necessarily reflect increased inclusivity in a wider sense. Rather, they reflected a changing conception of what an exclusive College was and how it should function. A small religious community on a strictly regulated schedule had become an obsolete ideal. While the idea of community remained a guiding principle, it took on new forms. New spaces, symbolised by the garden court and the freestanding library, speak of a new integration of architecture and nature as the ideal collegiate setting. Yet these spaces laid the foundation for further transformation, now seen in the greater openness of the College in all its aspects, and in setting an architectural tradition that continues to evolve in the new expansion across Trumpington Street.

2 The Architecture of Mill Lane

Beatie Blakemore

As the most significant transformation of the College since the fourteenth century, the Pembroke Mill Lane project was an unprecedented opportunity to expand the grounds of Pembroke directly adjacent to its foundational site. The scale of the Mill Lane site has enabled the College to create additional residential accommodation, as well as new spaces for a wide range of collegiate activities and operations. Perhaps most importantly, it has also provided space for new, public-facing activities including an Auditorium, foyer spaces and a publicly accessible exhibition space.

As architects, our challenge in developing the brief and designs for the site was to create a set of buildings and gardens that resonated with the existing College while also acknowledging the richly varied history of the Mill Lane site. We began by analysing the architecture and inhabitation of the historic College carefully, to develop an understanding of how the identity and ethos of Pembroke are embodied within its architecture and landscape.

Developed over 650 years of progressive expansion, the buildings of Pembroke are highly varied; each court displays individual characteristics of scale and architectural language reflective of its period. Yet overall the College still feels remarkably cohesive, in part through the recurring use of materials and motifs – deep red brick with stone dressings, articulated gables and the use of prominent chimney forms to lend vertical emphasis and modelling to the roofscape.

Pembroke is perhaps characterised most strongly by its distinctive landscape and gardens. The spaces between the buildings vary in scale and character, but are typified by open corners and diagonal views that connect each of the courts, visually layering the different periods of architectural development. As in many historic Colleges, the buildings are seldom connected internally. The external movement through the landscape is key to the experience of Pembroke;

The Library Lawn and the Wren Chapel. The tower of the former United Reformed Church, now Pembroke's new Auditorium, is behind.

the gardens act as the key connective tissue that links together the College's residential, social and academic life. Such movement is also an important part of the public experience of Pembroke, which – unusually for a Cambridge College – offers free access to its gardens and grounds.

The scale, intimacy and porosity of Pembroke's gardens became for us the key generating principle guiding the architectural interventions at Mill Lane. In reimagining how the existing site could be transformed into an expanded collegiate campus, we sought creatively to integrate new and historic elements around a series of connected open spaces that encourage interaction and support the communal life of the College.

Existing significant buildings have been carefully refurbished to accommodate new uses that enhance their architectural characteristics. New elements are designed to sit comfortably within the existing urban edges while framing new garden spaces in the centre of the site, opening up new views and connections to the existing buildings and the wider streetscape. The series of skilfully proportioned outdoor spaces extends the richness and variety of the existing College courts and gardens, yet also reinforces Pembroke's commitment to public access and welcome.

Haworth Tompkins, landscape plan – existing College and Mill Lane site.

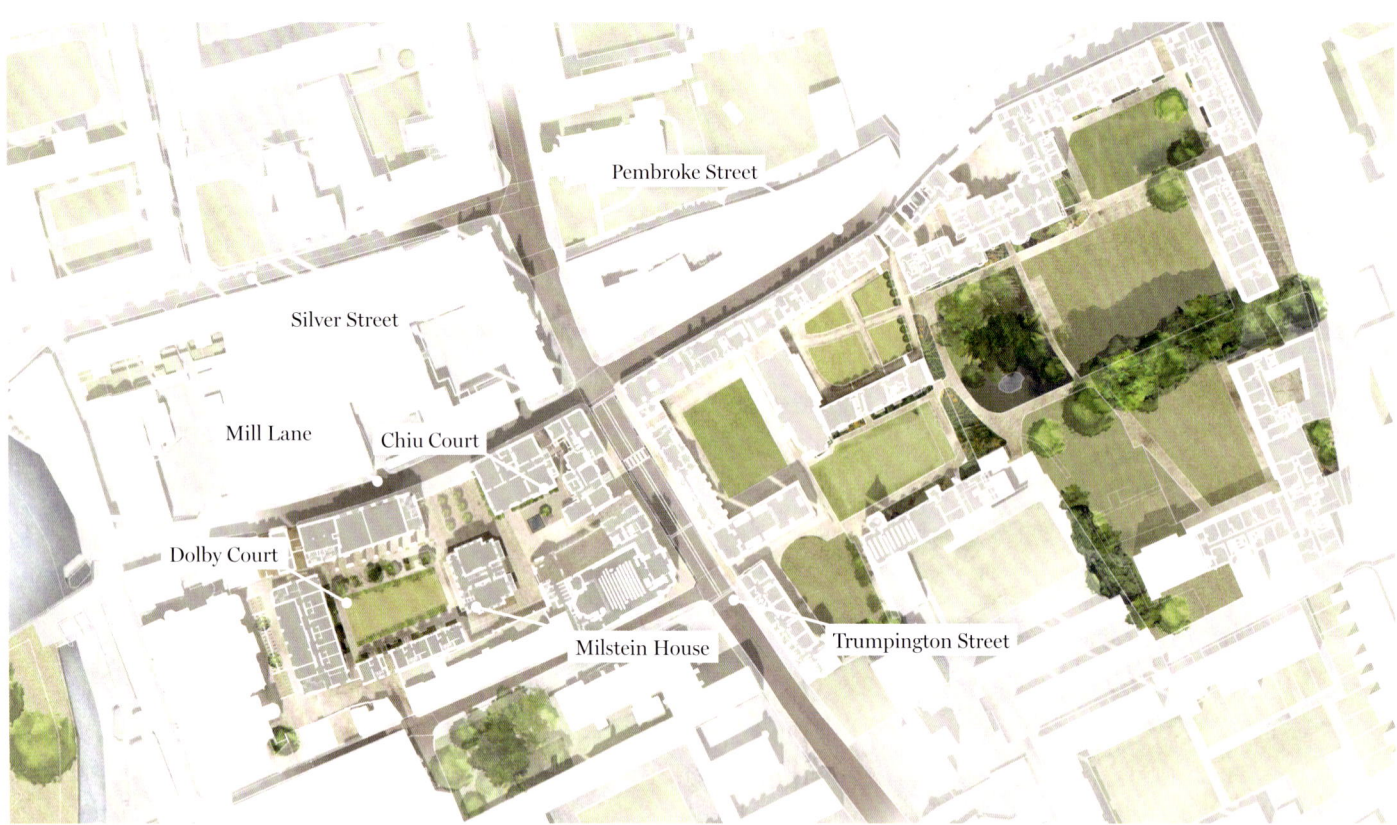

SITE ARRANGEMENT

At the heart of the site is Milstein House (formerly Stuart House), comprehensively refurbished to become a new social hub. Built in the 1920s, Stuart House was for many years home to the Cambridge Board of Extramural Studies; it subsequently accommodated the University Careers Service. The formal facades of the set-back, neo-Georgian building had become gradually overshadowed by later structures, among them the Lecture Block and rear extensions to 4 Mill Lane.

Now set within three new gardens, the building acts as the linchpin around which the new site is organised. Its handsome oak-lined interiors house not only new communal spaces for students, Fellows and staff, but also a Reading Room and Partnership Centre in which the College can foster new external relationships in academia and enterprise. The set-back facade to Mill Lane is now foregrounded by the new Blyth Garden, defined by a formal avenue of pollarded lime trees. To the west of Milstein House is the garden of the new Ray and Dagmar Dolby Court; to the east lies the new Chiu Court, around which the public and collegiate activities are arranged. This reflects the arrangement of the historic College in which the more private, residential areas are concentrated on its outer (eastern) edges, with social, collegiate and learning spaces clustered around a non-linear arrangement of semi-public courtyards and gardens.

Opposite The Auditorium, created out of the former United Reformed Church, seats 220 people. It is a magnificent venue for talks, lectures, concerts and music.

The new Gatehouse to the Mill Lane site (left) and 74 Trumpington Street (formerly Kenmare House).

ENTRANCE AND ARRIVAL

The main entrance to the expanded College site is marked by a new Gatehouse building on Trumpington Street. Taking the place of a three-storey warehouse dating from the late nineteenth century, it is a thoughtfully proportioned contemporary building which takes its place comfortably and confidently within the rich and diverse architectural ensemble of the street.

The new entrance building signals its collegiate identity through a recognisable affinity to the existing Pembroke buildings, while also acknowledging the non-collegiate history and character of the Mill Lane site. It does not seek to upstage the historic gateway to the existing College nor the formal frontage of Kenmare House (74 Trumpington Street), but rather to take its appropriate place within the spectrum of entrance points from the city.

The Gatehouse maintains the massing and prevailing line of the existing brick building that it replaces. In so doing it provides enclosure and framing to the adjacent Kenmare House. An arched passageway announces the new point of access to the Mill Lane site, giving direct views to Milstein House and the new foyer across Chiu Court. A secondary opening on the north-facing facade articulates the diagonal relationship with the existing Porters' Lodge. The covered passageway recalls the discreet scale and simple structural expression of the historic College entrance, while introducing the language of the expressed timber frame of the new foyer building beyond. The Gatehouse serves as both a threshold to the Mill Lane site and a public entrance to the range of accessible facilities clustered within this part of the College.

On the first floor of the new building is a public exhibition room, offering space both for the display of College treasures and collaborative exhibitions with the University and local artists. The relationship to the existing College is reinforced by a large window onto Trumpington Street, its scale echoing that of the windows on the three expressed gables of the Chapel, Old Library and First Court. As in the existing College, this acts as an urban signifier of the more communal activities within, communicating the public nature of the space.

AUDITORIUM AND FOYERS

On the ground floor, the new Gatehouse building connects to a complex sequence of public and collegiate foyer spaces, designed to support the Auditorium. The Auditorium is a new facility for Pembroke and the wider city, providing a flexible, technically equipped space for a range of uses: performance and recitals, speaker events and panel discussions, as well as University lectures.

The primary foyer is conceived as a simple, beautifully proportioned space enclosed by an

Chiu Court from the foyer; light and space from the courtyard is brought into the new building.

Chiu Court, with the foyer and Auditorium behind: a mix of architecture from the eighteenth, nineteenth and twenty-first centuries.

expressed timber frame. In plan, the building describes a subtle arc between the existing masonry structures of 76 Trumpington Street, the former church and the former School Hall. The single-storey building is carefully scaled to open up views from the new Chiu Court towards the side elevation of the Auditorium. The original stonework is illuminated by a linear rooflight that recalls the external passageway that historically led to the former Church School House. The School House itself has been carefully reconstructed using reclaimed bricks from the original building to form a new, two-storey social space accommodating a mezzanine study area, WCs and a bar. Together, these spaces will support a range of new public, collegiate and University activities in the Auditorium.

Within the foyer building are two new works by the artist Alison Turnbull, who was commissioned by the College to lead a series of public art interventions across the new site. The paintings have a formal and thematic relationship with Turnbull's landscape work within Chiu Court, carried out in collaboration with the design team at Tom Stuart-Smith.

CHIU COURT

The new garden of Chiu Court is enclosed by an informal ensemble of new and historic buildings. These now house a range of functions including administrative offices and teaching facilities. In creating the new garden we sought to give clarity and prominence to the most significant historic buildings by selectively removing intrusive elements, and skilfully carefully interweaving new architectural interventions.

Within the existing buildings, internal spaces were restored to their original proportions and the fabric carefully refurbished to improve environmental and acoustic performance. The new interventions have radically improved the energy efficiency of the historic buildings, forming part of a holistic sustainability strategy for the site as a whole.

RAY AND DAGMAR DOLBY COURT

The second phase of the development has delivered the first new residential court for Pembroke in a quarter of a century, providing a series of intimate personal study and dwelling spaces arranged around a beautifully landscaped garden. Enclosed by three new buildings as well as the partially retained Millers Yard building, Dolby Court is of a scale recognisable to the College. The distinct Pembroke character of interconnected gardens bound by buildings of varying height and massing is reflected in the new court; each building is designed to respond to the specific conditions at the site's edges.

The retained front building of the former Millers Yard has been comprehensively refurbished and extended to accommodate new student bedrooms addressing Mill Lane. This building also houses shared student facilities such as a new gym and a laundry.

Adjacent and to the rear of this building are two new residential buildings form the northern and western edges of the new court. These dual-aspect buildings present four storeys to both Mill Lane and Dolby Court; a crenellated top storey is defined by bay windows that step back from the building edge. The new buildings provide generously scaled ensuite bedrooms in intimate community clusters of up to six bedrooms, which share large kitchens overlooking the new court. Connected internally via naturally lit corridors, all rooms are fully lift-accessible and the buildings include a number of purpose-designed

rooms for wheelchair users, as well as lateral sets for Fellows and guests.

To the southern edge of the court is a lower, three-storey building, its scale responding to that of the neighbouring residential building along Little St Mary's Lane. This building is configured in a traditional College staircase arrangement, with accessible bedrooms and kitchens on the ground floor and ensuite bedrooms above.

MATERIALS AND SURFACE ARTICULATION

The material language of the new buildings responds to the existing palette of both the College and Mill Lane sites. It is typified by loadbearing red or gault brick in lime mortar, with reconstituted-stone window surrounds. A consistent material and compositional language has been adopted for each of the blocks, but have with in the window sizes and fenestration in response to the rooms' internal arrangement and orientation.

Bedrooms on the ground, first and second floors include a large central window with reconstituted-stone surrounds and a central stone mullion, providing additional shading to the windows facing west and south. The depth of the window reveals is also increased here to minimise solar gain and to introduce subtle variation in the degree of surface modelling across the facades.

On the third floor, the volumetric form of the bay windows introduces a vertical emphasis that recalls the rhythm of chimneys along the existing College's northern edge. This is particularly apparent in the long view on approach down Mill Lane.

Due to the set-back position of Milstein House, the gable end of the new building on Mill Lane also plays an important urban role.

The magnificent exhibition space created above the new gatehouse leading from Trumpington Street. Its innovative design showcases the things of value that Pembroke has and does.

The gable is defined by a prominent ventilation chimney and the expressed form of the corner stair, featuring a triptych window lantern that looks towards the historic College on Pembroke Street. On approach from the river, the scale of the new building and its rigorous composition of openings sits confidently within the existing urban grain of Mill Lane. It also maintains the consistency in material yet variety in scale that is characteristic of buildings in the area.

Opposite *4 Mill Lane, renovated to become a learning centre, now offers teaching, meeting and seminar rooms.*

The new south block of Dolby Court, designed to mirror the staircase format of the historic College.

GARDENS

Within Dolby Court, the new garden is designed to feel intimate, inviting and beautifully planted, drawing on the range of landscape precedents within the existing College. The Court itself is an actively used space, in which perimeter planting and changes in level encourage people to sit and linger.

The compositional formality of the blocks will be further softened by the introduction of planting to the buildings' edges. Such planting includes climbing plants as well as deep flower beds to provide an abundance of seasonal colour and variety.

ENVIRONMENTAL DESIGN

The new buildings are designed to BREEAM Excellent standard and adopt the principles of passive environmental design to reduce energy consumption and carbon emissions. This includes deep window reveals to reduce solar gain; natural ventilation through large, opening windows; high thermal mass through plastered concrete soffits; and high levels of insulation and air tightness. Heating will be provided through air-source heat pumps, which will also enable cooling during the hottest months via cast-in pipework to the slabs. Solar photovoltaic

The balcony above the foyer building is a space for rest and study, as well as for receptions associated with events in the Auditorium. The stained glass is by Ardyn Halter, a Pembroke alumnus.

Below *Detailing of the staircases in the west and north blocks of Dolby Court has been carefully finished.*

panels on both new and existing roofs facilitate on-site generation of electricity, supporting an entirely gas-free site.

The buildings feature load-bearing lime-mortared brickwork, recycled copper alloy roof coverings and an internal concrete frame, designed are designed for longevity over time and to allow future adaptability in the configuration or use of the rooms. The simple material palette of internal finishes, including oak joinery and engineered oak floorboards, has been selected to age and patinate gracefully through future generations of use and inhabitation.

3 Acquiring the Mill Lane Site

Andrew Cates

The opportunity to extend the medieval domus of a central Cambridge College only presents itself once every century or two. For decades Pembroke had been coveting the shambolic collection of buildings on the Mill Lane site. Of course the land plot, including both sides of Mill Lane, also abuts three other Colleges (four if you include Peterhouse in two corners), all with their own hopes and aspirations. The site was certainly a mess, comprising some 54 buildings of different ages. Most of the land, though, rested in the hands of the University. No official of any institution relishes the risk, however remote, of being considered responsible for the sale of their respective Crown Jewels.

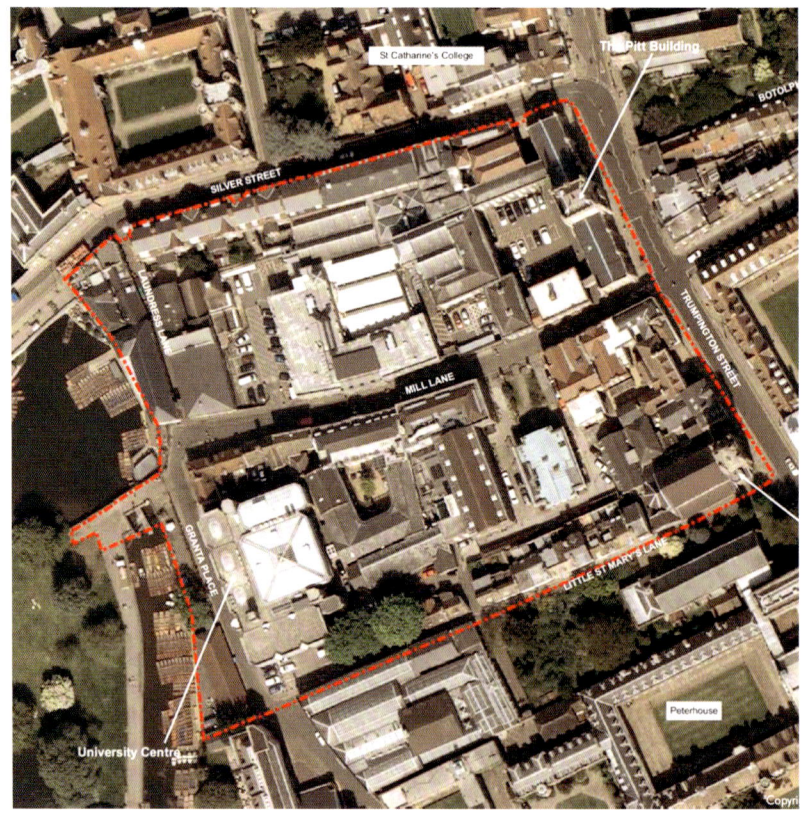

An aerial map from the 'Supplementary Planning Document', showing both the north and south sides of Mill Lane, looking from the river. Pembroke's site, on the south (right) side, reveals the awkward jumble of original buildings.

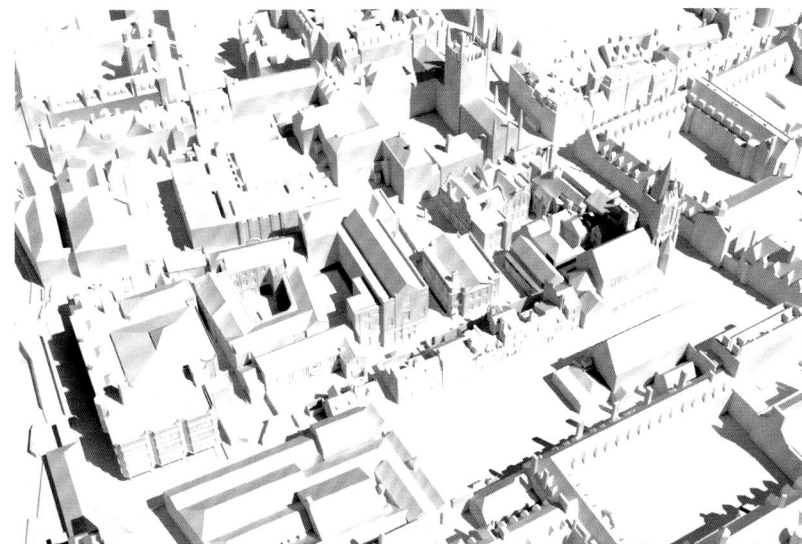

*Two models of the Mill Lane site.
Above: the Mill Lane site as it was.
Below: the site as it now is.*

The myriad committees of the University rarely move on anything before they have to. As the aerial photograph shows the southern half of the site (to the right) resembled an upturned carton of Lego bricks, and the northern half (to the left) dense factory buildings. This could have carried on for decades more. However, the City Council had ideas of improvement. In January 2010 it issued a 'Supplementary Planning Document', declaring that the entire site on the north and south of Mill Lane, including the Old Press Site, was ripe for redevelopment but that no development would be permitted before a Masterplan was agreed. To complicate the situation further, this was also a conservation area with many listed buildings. Nonetheless, excitement among the Colleges rose. The aerial photograph shows the red line of the planning zone.

THE OLD MILLERS YARD

The first point of leverage emerged when the old Millers Yard, part of the old city industrial heritage, was put on the market by an investment company at full price. Ownership of this building was a crucial pawn because it divided the site; without owning it, the University could not easily develop a grand sitewide scheme. In a spirit of collegiate unity, four Colleges – Pembroke, Darwin, St Catharine's and Queens' – bought Millers Yard together in 2012. Peterhouse declared itself not interested. The University did nothing, but looked on with disapproval.

The Colleges, advised by the late Andrew Chadwick, a Pembroke alumnus, decided on a risky plan. If planning consent was granted on a plausible use for Millers Yard, it would be very hard to overturn this subsequently with a scheme that developed the whole site because retaining buildings in a conservation area where possible is an established objective; industrial heritage in Cambridge is also rare. The Colleges thus applied to develop Millers Yard into a student residential block, separating the University Centre from the Mill Lane Lecture Block. When the application was submitted, the University suddenly took notice. They objected on a technicality and simultaneously approached the Colleges directly to request withdrawal of the plans before consideration. They had blinked first.

And so, inch-by-inch, the shaping of ideas began. Several threads were running in parallel; years of negotiation between the Colleges and the University on what the Masterplan would look like, which parts the University would keep and which parts the Colleges would develop, as well as when the development might happen. A contractual negotiation on the terms of any purchase proceeded, while an entirely separate discussion took place between the Colleges on how the site might be divided up. Steady dialogue with the city planners was also needed.

Agreement between the Colleges was fairly easy to obtain and good faith abounded, trust having been built up over years of partnership – even though the site was always going to struggle to meet everyone's aspirations. It was agreed upfront that each College would pay pro-rata for its share of the site based on land area. Initially the north side was considered the better real estate, with demolition much more likely and the possibility for unencumbered development. The south side was split neatly in two by the existing Stuart House (now Milstein House); it also had frontage buildings to the north, east and south, which would need to be largely retained.

Pembroke was initially allocated the northeast quarter of the site behind the Pitt Building, with the hope of eventually purchasing that separately. The College had historical associations with this area, having turned down the Pitt Building back in the Victorian era. When the Pitt acquisition was researched and looked impossible in prospect, Pembroke's flag was moved to the quarter of the site closest to the College, the Mill Lane lecture block. The College then started a long discussion with the University about adding 74 Trumpington Street and 1 and 4 Mill Lane as a separate purchase.

The nineteenth-century 4 Mill Lane building with handsome Dutch gables served for many years as the home of the Board of Graduate Studies. Many a completed PhD thesis has been posted through the letterbox to the right of the door.

THE ROLE OF THE OLD SCHOOLS

Meanwhile, discussion with the University regarding the Masterplan (aided by architects and urban planners Allies and Morrison) was complicated by a belief on the part of the Old Schools that they badly needed to own commercial space in Cambridge; they believed that they should therefore retain part of the site to let as retail outlets. That this site was a miserable walk from anywhere to park all winter was brushed over, and the Old Schools insisted on plans with the whole of the ground floor of the north site, always regarded as the premium part of the site, given over to some 3,000 sq. m (32,292 sq. ft) of retail. (They were also oblivious to the approaching decline of physical retail in the face of online sales.)

The north half of the site appeared in danger of changing from College courtyards to 'rooms over a shop' – or alternatively structures very expensive to build because of the need to create 'floating' courtyards sealed off from retail below. On the south side the University eventually accepted only 300 sq. m (3,229 sq. ft) of shops, fronting on to Mill Lane. Pressure from a desire to commit timing to the Dolby family allowed Pembroke and Darwin to push ahead with the south side as the negotiation on the north side slowed down. Although the south side now looked the more attractive prospect, with more buildings around it and no retail beneath, the site was split on a pro-rata land area basis. The north side eventually failed, but not before Queens' College had obtained further concessions from the University on lease length and price.

But how to price a land transaction between the Colleges and the University? Both sets of trustees have an obligation to achieve value for money, but buildings changing hands was somewhat unique. Andrew Chadwick wrote a careful, good-faith paper in 2013 suggesting a basis for a 'fair and equitable price'. The University responded by appointing retail estate advisors who characterised it as a 'horse sale' and tried to justify roughly double the price on the basis of potential returns from a 'market plan', filling the space with small, cheap student housing and letting it out at exorbitant prices to Anglia Ruskin students. Three years of discussion later, following a series of offers and counter-offers, and after a confusing hokey-cokey on what was and was not included and the agreed price, on a like for like basis the eventual deal almost matched Chadwick's original suggestion to a penny. The University negotiators retired, having perhaps learned that while being demanding is often fruitful, being difficult is not.

EMMANUEL CHURCH BUILDINGS

Meanwhile another narrative was coming together at the southeast corner of the site. Some elders from Emmanuel Church came to see the bursar to explain that since 1972, when the Congregational Church and Presbyterian Church had merged, the United Reformed Church had occupied two church buildings very close together in central Cambridge. The logic of merging congregations had always been strong, and was increasing with current demographics. However, the congregation would need to decide collectively and might be persuaded by a once-in-a-lifetime opportunity. Was it possible to approach them with a sufficiently attractive offer? The College Meeting, recalling the rarity of freehold adjacent to the site, jumped at the opportunity and dispatched the bursar to negotiate.

This produced another tricky pricing issue. If the church building was valued based on income from rental and the collection plate minus heating and maintenance costs, it would only be worth £100,000; the cost to build it (as we discovered when it came to insuring it) would be around £47 million. Other valuation methods, unsurprisingly, gave answers in between. Churches have sold for nothing and for small fortunes, depending on how they could be developed. What would be a fair price? This time the approach was much more collaborative. Within a couple of months a settlement of £4.5 million had been reached for the Church and Hall (with a further contribution for 1 Little St Mary's Lane). As a freehold sale there were few sticking points, and over time the congregation even decided not to attempt to move their organ or any of the historical plaques.

Next Darwin, with other projects in prospect, suggested that they might trade off their moral rights to the southwest corner of the site in return for a 30-year agreement to accommodate some of their students. The makings of a spectacular development running from Trumpington Street down to the University

A view of Pembroke's Auditorium. The pulpit from the original United Reformed Church has been kept, but there is now a new stage, new seating, new lighting and new heating.

Two preliminary sketches of the Dolby Court site from the original Allies & Morrison masterplan, illustrating alternative approaches to the potential scale of the new development, showing how the removal of the Mill Lane lecture block could open up the site.

Centre was now coming together. However, all of the purchases needed to be negotiated, and right in the middle was Stuart House (now Milstein House) – with plans already drawn up for its conversion to a new centre for the Gates Scholars (displaced from the University Centre).

The difference between a whole site and two halves was profound. Even access and security for others right into the middle of a College site was a challenge. Time for the Vice Chancellor and Master to disappear into a smoke-filled room. Then a handshake was done, perhaps the only part of the site where a building changed hands with Pembroke paying a little strategic premium. In a single stroke the south side of Mill Lane, previously the less attractive side, suddenly felt like a whole site, unencumbered by the ground-floor retail requirements on the north.

COMPLETION OF THE SITE

Now a new vision could unfold. The existing plans had been constructed as part of the sale negotiation. The College (by Parlour consultation, including Emeritus Fellows) strongly supported a strategy of 'demassing' the site, reducing the number of rooms and buildings in order for it to 'feel' more like the rest of the College's historic site. In order to create Dolby Court into a Pembroke-style open court, 40 bedrooms were lost. However, adding a floor on to the Orchard Building would feel better than cramming the new site.

The final chapter in the acquisition of the site came when the University not only withdrew from the north side negotiations but also declared it no longer wanted to retain any commercial interest on the south side. By this stage a new and more decisive University team was in place and they quickly determined reasonable terms for the change. Planning terms were fixed for two units facing on to Mill Lane for the College to manage; the third could be changed into a much-needed gym, free-weights room and changing rooms. Our site was now complete.

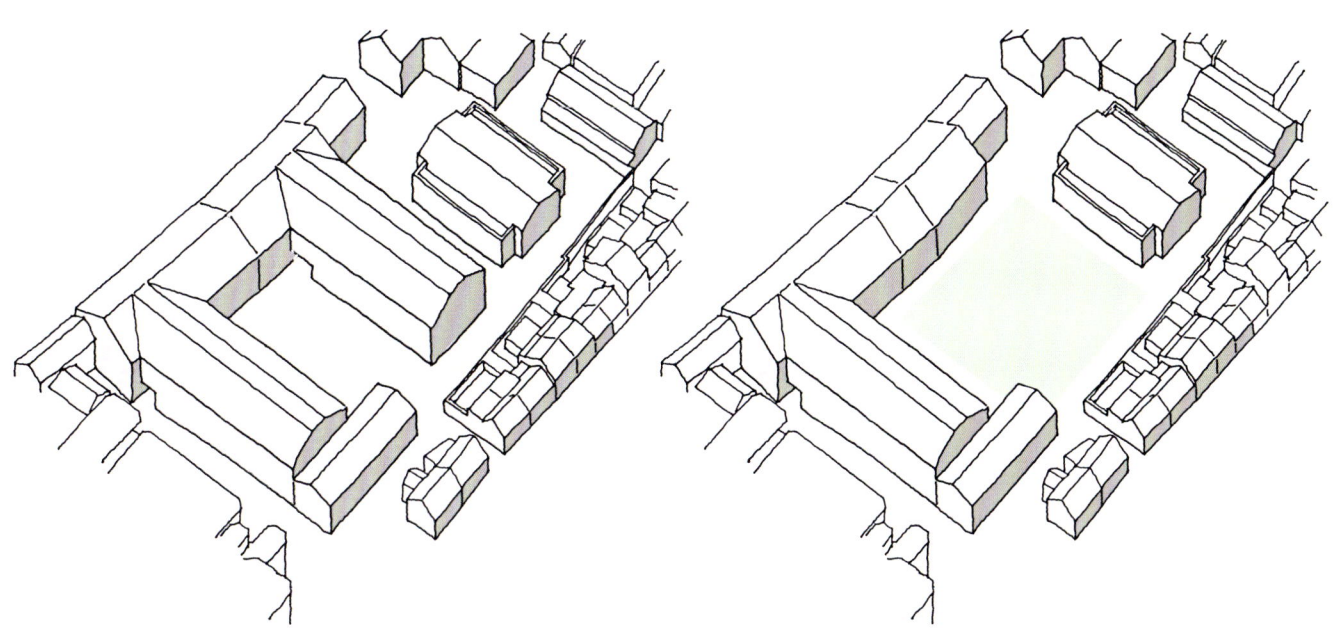

Part II
Ray Dolby and his Legacy

4 Ray Dolby at Cambridge

Dagmar Dolby

My late husband, Ray Dolby, spent six rewarding years at Pembroke College, Cambridge, from 1957 to 1963, during which time he earned his PhD. It was for Ray the culmination of a brilliant education in the sciences and the arts, as well as a portal to a professional career that combined his passion for scientific exploration, his innovations with practical technology and his creation of a successful business enterprise. Searching for solutions to difficult problems was what he loved most. At Cambridge he was able to hone these skills, leading him to the career that would make Dolby a household name.

Ray was born in 1933 in Portland, Oregon, where his parents lived at the time, trying to make a living in the midst of the Great Depression. After the Second World War his family found themselves in the San Francisco Bay area, where during his high-school years Ray came into contact with technology in the earliest days of Silicon Valley. While still in high school, and then

Previous spread
The new Foyer, created in beautiful brick and wood immediately beside the Auditorium, is for mingling, meeting and study; on the wall is Alison Turnbull's work, Up and Down in the Void.

Left *Ray Dolby at Pembroke, where he arrived as a PhD student in 1957. He later became a Research Fellow at the College.*

Looking into Old Court from Ray Dolby's old room on E staircase. It is now known as the Christopher Smart Room.

at College, Ray was one of several key members of the team at Ampex Corporation that developed the first video-tape recorder. While he could have continued working at Ampex and foregone getting a college degree, his parents had instilled in him the importance of an education. Ray took their world-view to heart and became the first member of his family to earn a college degree.

Ray graduated from Stanford University in 1957. He won a Marshall Scholarship, one of 12 awarded in the United States and one of only four allotted to the country's Western Region. Along with the other scholars, he sailed across the Atlantic on the *Queen Elizabeth*. Even though Ray had travelled all over the United States, as well as briefly to Mexico, it was his first experience of Europe. Fortunately, after reading extensively about the UK and studying its literature, Ray felt at home as soon as he arrived in England. It was very important to him to fall in with the customs and etiquette of the British, and not appear at all to be what he would call 'an ugly American'.

He was assigned to Pembroke College for his two years of study, where he planned to take Part II of the Tripos in Mechanical Sciences. He quickly realised that he had already exceeded this level of study as an undergraduate, and so he received permission to embark straightaway on a PhD programme. When it came to choosing the subject for his doctoral thesis, he explored the computer department, the radio astronomy department and the area of electronics. He finally settled on the field of electron and X-ray microscopy.

In his first two years, Ray spent more time at the Cavendish Laboratory than he did in the College. This was not the present-day Cavendish, out to the west of the university, but the 'old'

Cavendish on Free School Lane, just a stone's throw from Pembroke College. The motto of the Cavendish, and of Cambridge's Department of Physics, is deceptively simple: 'Physics is what physicists do'. Ray appreciated how the Cavendish Laboratory sought out the world's finest researchers and supported their scientific pursuits wherever they cared to venture.

Ray's interest was piqued by long-wavelength X-rays. In consultation with Dr V.E. Cosslett, who became his supervisor, he embarked on a research programme that sought to detect and analyse extremely long-wavelength X-rays – including, for example, elements such as carbon or aluminium. The exploration of long-wavelength X-rays had previously been discarded, as they were seen as being extremely weak. However, Ray found this intriguing and chose it for his PhD programme. It was an original course of study that had not previously been explored.

In his free time Ray enjoyed music, among other hobbies. He started brushing up on his clarinet-playing skills from high school when he heard that Newnham, an all-female College, needed a clarinettist for its orchestra. He improved his clarinet playing and also opened up new avenues of his social life.

When the Cambridge University Tape Recording Society discovered that Ray had a superb recording set-up in his rooms, including a rare Ampex tape recorder and professional microphones, he was swiftly invited to join the society. Ray's rooms in the College were in the first court and adjacent to the old chapel. This meant that he could lay microphone lines across the roof and record some of the magnificent music that was performed there with regularity.

Ray's interest in music and recording led him indeed to his eventual professional pursuits. In those early days, he found that there was an excellent signal-to-noise ratio in the signal coming directly from the chapel, but he could immediately hear the deterioration when he switched to the output of the tape recorder. The before-signal was glorious. However, even with a good machine like the $7\frac{1}{2}$ IPS two-track Ampex, the result was less impressive. This experience set him thinking about recording systems and how he could improve them.

Ray's work at the Cavendish led to any number of publications, as well as conferences all over Europe – and even in the then Soviet Union, a remarkable experience for an American in the middle of the Cold War. He loved travelling on the continent and also tracked down the villages in Finland from which his maternal grandparents had emigrated to the United States before the turn of the nineteenth century.

In 1963 Ray Dolby gifted a magnificent silver jug to Pembroke. The College crest is engraved on the front.

Ray and Dagmar Dolby in 2012. Ray and Dagmar met in Cambridge when Ray was at Pembroke and Dagmar attending an English language course. Their second meeting occurred by chance, just outside the Mill pub – a stone's throw away from where the Ray and Dagmar Dolby Court now stands.

Upon completion of his thesis 'Long Wavelength X-ray Microanalysis' and his oral examination in December 1961, Ray was awarded his PhD in Physics. More than a year earlier, he had been appointed to a Junior Research Fellowship at Pembroke, giving him special status within the College. The life of a Cambridge Fellow was replete with creature comforts, including dinners at High Table and erudite discussions with other scholars (amply lubricated by port in the Senior Parlour). Ray was also provided with an apartment in the College, attended to by a respectful staff of retainers. In a letter home to his old mentor, he described his living room as the most beautiful room at Cambridge. Located in the oldest part of the College, it dated from about 1350; new oak panelling had been added in 1630. However, he did have to get used to the lack of a proper bathroom in the old building. This meant that he had to walk a distance to a newer part of the College for his daily shower.

The rooms were large enough to accommodate an entire jazz band, allowing Ray to have some wonderful moments in E5. At the same time he was expected to carry out certain duties as a Junior Fellow, including conducting an audit of the College's silver, going back to its founding in 1347. Ray was very conscious of the unusual nature of life as a Fellow at the College, writing that,

> The whole system is looked at with a critical eye from time to time, but Cambridge, being the conservative place it is, is unlikely to change very fast. It is an ancient system; ancient systems, unless decisively proved otherwise, are likely to be considered right.

I would be remiss if I did not mention that the most important event of my life happened right here in Cambridge on 17 June 1962. Ray and I, who had briefly met at an event the night before, ran into each other in front of the Mill pub. A hello turned into a conversation, then a party invitation, and then into a relationship for the rest of my time at Cambridge – which was only a few weeks, as I was there for an English language course.

We were married in 1966 and lived in London for ten years, where Ray started Dolby Laboratories. Here we lived through the trials of the fledgling company before moving our family and the company to San Francisco in 1976. Despite his decision to move back to the United States, Ray never forgot the value of his time at Cambridge. He would often speak fondly of his experiences there and was forever grateful for the role that the University had played in his life.

5 The History of the Mill Lane Site

Chris Blencowe

The Mill Lane quarter of Cambridge has a long and varied history. The lane served as a link between the busy thoroughfare of what is now Trumpington Street and the important riverside Bishop's and King's Mills. It roughly followed the line of the King's Ditch, which marked the historic outer limits of Cambridge and served as a sometime sewer, running between the thirteenth-century Trumpington Gate and the River Cam. While much of the rest of the city was gradually populated with grander University and College buildings, Mill Lane remained very much a 'town' area for many centuries. It was fronted by a few substantial houses on Trumpington Street, with a mixture of open space and commercial and residential properties running down towards the river. As the influence of river traffic waned, buildings came and went. Their uses also changed. There is possible evidence of a brewery on the site of Millers Yard in earlier centuries, as well as a sprinkling of public

4 Mill Lane in 1886, when it was originally created as a purpose-built central office for the Local Examination Syndicate, now Cambridge Assessment.

Chiu Court with 4 Mill Lane and the rear of 74 Trumpington Street (formerly Kenmare House). Here buildings from the eighteenth and nineteenth centuries are complemented by a contemporary courtyard.

houses and small enterprises. There are even tales of a minor red-light district.

During the nineteenth century the University expanded into this part of the city. The process started with development of the Pitt Building and University Press on the northern side of the lane, followed by the acquisition of 1 Mill Lane and the construction of its neighbour at no. 4. By this time an elegant set of formal frontages marked the Trumpington Street/Mill Lane corner. A sizeable garden behind Kenmare House also added character. Towards the river, by contrast, the site comprised a much denser grain of narrow lanes and courtyards, with tightly packed housing and a variety of commercial activities.

The University presence was strengthened during the twentieth century with the construction of Stuart House, the University Lecture Block and, eventually, the University Centre in the 1960s. Despite these developments, the area lacked coherent identity. By the beginning of the twenty-first century it had become rather neglected, disjointed and generally down-at-heel.

Nevertheless, the site contained some handsome listed buildings and a few other, perhaps less worthy, non-designated heritage assets. Principal among these is the Grade II-listed United Reformed Church, opened in 1874 as the Emmanuel Congregational

5 THE HISTORY OF THE MILL LANE SITE

Left *An aerial view of Pembroke College and the Mill Lane site, as they were in 1920.*

Opposite *Little St Mary's Lane. In the foreground is no. 5, the Half Moon Pub and subsequently a house of some ill repute. It is now owned by Pembroke and occupied by students.*

Church and designed by James Cubitt in the Modified Early English style. The tightness of its chosen site explains the design of a long, single-space nave. The scale and the inclusion of schoolrooms shows the new-found confidence of the congregationalists following the removal of religious restrictions on students with the passing of the University Test Act in 1871. Their ambition was reflected in the plans for nearly 700 seats in the church, as well as the landmark tower, standing in contrast to the lower, nearby and much older Established Church buildings of Pembroke Chapel and St Mary the Less.

Some of the congregation may have taken satisfaction that the Georgian-style buildings demolished to build the church included the Half Moon Pub. If so, the feeling was probably short-lived, as the pub soon reappeared further down Little St Mary's Lane at no. 5. Here, in the 1920s, it acquired a very colourful and controversial reputation under the owner and host Noel Teulon-Porter.

The block of buildings known as Kenmare House (comprising of 74 and 74a Trumpington Street and 1 Mill Lane) are Grade II-listed as a single block. Though built at different times, they all sit on the former site of a medieval manor called Cotton Hall, purchased by John Randall in 1768 and modernised by local architect James Essex. Reputed to be one of Georgian England's leading provincial architects, Essex set about refashioning the house by refronting and remodelling the building in the style of the time. By 1830 the house had gained an extension to the rear and 1 Mill Lane had also been built. Shortly after, 74a was added.

The buildings were acquired by the University in 1892, with 74a becoming the home of the Cambridge University Appointments Association and its successor, the Appointments Board. The rest of the buildings, as well as nos 75 and 76, were let to small businesses and a boarding house, run by a Mrs Elizabeth Johnson. In 1906 she convinced the University

to build a two-storey addition on the end of the previous nineteenth-century rear extension. A small infill development was constructed in 1929 between 1 and 4 Mill Lane, the latter also to acquire an extension to its rear.

Looking back on 250 years of incremental development, it is clear that much attention was given to the frontages of the buildings. These provided a handsome streetscape on the extended corner of Trumpington Street and Mill Lane. Behind, however, an unimpressive mixture of later, ad hoc additions were incrementally built on what had once been a spacious garden.

Fronting this once green space on its northern side lies 4 Mill Lane. Despite its history and stylish Dutch pedimented gables, the building is neither listed nor identified by the Council as a Building of Local Interest. Maps of the sixteenth century show the site as open ground. However, by the time of Loggan's 1690 map (p. 16), there is evidence of a T-shaped building with a large garden area to the rear, presumably that of John Randall's new house (later Kenmare House). On the Mill Lane side of the site, the King's Ditch linked the newly built Hobson's Conduit with the Mill Pond; several small bridges also crossed the lane.

The present building was built in 1886 and designed by W.M. Fawcett, an eminent local architect whose other work includes the Wileman Building (originally the Training College for Women) at Hughes Hall and the Friars Building at Queens' College. It was originally built to house the expanding work of the Local Examination Syndicate, also responsible for local lectures. Seven years later it was extended, under Fawcett's guidance, to provide additional space. Before long the

The jumble of original buildings in what is now Chin Court. The United Reformed Church, dating from 1874, is to the right of the site.

58   PEMBROKE COLLEGE, CAMBRIDGE THE BUILDINGS AND GARDENS

Syndicate had outgrown this extended building too. It separated its local lecture responsibilities from the examinations by establishing the Board of Extramural Studies in the newly built Stuart House, which opened in 1927.

The site of Stuart House is formed by a portion of the former gardens of Kenmare House and the yard and workshops of William Sindall – a builder who also become one of the major contractors for the subsequent work. The house is named after James Stuart, the founding secretary of the Syndicate. It was commissioned following the Royal Commission on Oxford and Cambridge Universities, which recommended:

> the establishment of a Centre or House for extra-mural studies, in as central a position as possible ... consisting of the necessary administrative offices and of accommodation for the existing libraries, and for students wishing to read or write there. (Stuart House Opening Brochure 1927)

It has been designated by the local planning authority as a Building of Local Interest – not only for its elegant revived Georgian (or neo-Mary and William) style, but also as the culmination of the previous 50 years' work by the various guises of the Board of Extramural Studies. Latterly it served for over 40 years as the University's Careers Service. The house was designed by George Hubbard, who was heavily engaged in most aspects of the building. According to the 1927 Opening Brochure:

> he designed not only the building as a whole, but the wrought-iron gates and railings, the University arms in the pediment, the memorial tablet, the shelving in the library, the clock faces, the panelling, tables and chairs in the Board room, the bookcase and cupboard in the secretary's room.

The result was one of a coherent building and fittings, described at the time as being 'sumptuously appointed'.

To the rear of Stuart House, at 6 Little St Mary's Lane, is the former home of Stephen and Jane Hawking. The family lived here for several years in the early 1970s until, with their family growing and Professor Hawking's condition worsening, they moved to a Gonville and Caius property on West Road. Testament to their time at 6 is provided by what has become known as the Hawking Door. This still gives access through their back yard onto the Mill Lane site, and onwards to Stephen Hawking's former office in the Department for Applied Mathematics and Theoretical Physics on the north side of Mill Lane.

Two larger buildings have been demolished to enable the construction of Dolby Court. Neither were listed nor identified by the City Council as Buildings of Local Interest. The Bailey, Grundy, Barrett Building, built in 1899 to house this electrical company's warehouse, was a medium-scale construction, tucked away in the southwest corner of the site. It was used by the company until 1973, then subsequently by the University's Estate Management organisation until 2017. The University Lecture Block occupied a far more prominent position, however, and was constructed on a much larger scale. Built as the Literary Lecture Rooms between 1931 and 1933, it was designed by Arnold Dunbar-Smith and modified in the 1950s to provide greater capacity. It loomed over its neighbouring buildings and its position, tight to the pavement, contrasted strongly with the generous space and set-piece design of Stuart House.

Opinions over the merits of the Lecture Block varied. T.C. Hughes, in an edition of *The Builder* published shortly after the Lecture Block's construction, noted that its tall front of Sussex brick was slightly concave, lending 'untold dignity and mystery to the building'. Nikolaus Pevsner was far less complimentary, however. His *Architectural Guide to Cambridgeshire* described it as 'frankly utilitarian' in 2002 and, worse still, as 'a disappointing performance by A. Dunbar-Smith' in the 2014 edition.

Unlike its more imposing neighbour at 4 Mill Lane, Millers Yard was included in the City Council's list of Buildings of Local Interest. This particular entry may owe more to a nostalgic view of what, towards the end of the twentieth century, had been a vibrant courtyard containing a restaurant and offices, but which by the mid-2010s had become empty and run down. Some local historians believe that the site once housed a brewery, but this is disputed. However, there is evidence over the centuries of offices associated with the neighbouring mills, residential dwellings and even a billiard hall.

What is evident is that it did not exist in anything like its late twentieth-century form before the Eden Lilley department store rebuilt it in 1903 and added further significant modifications in 1925. Very little of the original fabric was retained during these changes, as the store sought to provide space for workshops, stabling, storage and, eventually, its undertaker's business. The Yard's final major alteration came between 1983 and 1985, when substantial modification to the inner court, significant changes to the height and design of the facade, and the addition of twentieth-century gates

Looking from Dolby Court towards the old Pitt Building, framed by the new north range of the Court and Milstein House.

provided what was in reality a 1980s interpretation of a Victorian industrial building. The largely retained facade, now incorporated into the northern block of Dolby Court, thus speaks more of nostalgia than it does of architectural history.

At 12 Mill Lane, Adrienne Weil set up a graduate lodging house in 1942. Here Rosalind Franklin, the pioneering chemist, crystallographer and contributor to the discovery of DNA, lived at the end of her fourth year of studies at Cambridge. In 1962 it became the Women's Graduate Club.

THE PROCESS OF PLANNING

Gaining detailed planning approval was always going to be a long and complex process. Sitting in the historic core of Cambridge, part of a large conservation area, any development on this large site, with its Grade II-listed buildings and others designated as being of Local Interest, would generate a great deal of scrutiny from the Council's team of heritage officers, as well as a variety of local organisations with preservation interests. Almost everyone agreed that the site needed to be redeveloped. However, it was going to take quite an effort to convince the city that what Pembroke was planning respected not

The landscape architect Tom Stuart-Smith's sketch of Blyth Gardens (2017) is an aerial sketch looking south from Mill Lane, showing pollarded lime trees framing the façade of Milstein House.

only the significant buildings, but would also provide a site with an enhanced and coherent character.

The Council's 'Supplementary Planning Document', had been published in January 2010. It covered the larger site, including the riverfront and north side of Mill Lane. The Document opened the possibility for student accommodation and called for the preservation and/or enhancement of the area through the adaptive use of existing buildings where possible, together with the provision of high-quality, sustainable new buildings of innovative design. Another important requirement was to open up the site by improving permeability and creating lines of visibility into any new development. While the College was confident that our aspirations would meet these requirements, it would take a good deal of work to convince the planners and heritage officers in City Hall. For them, Mill Lane was one of the last major development opportunities within the historic core – and experience had left them with a healthy suspicion of developers.

Looking from the new Trumpington Street Gatehouse into Chiu Court and Milstein House.

From the start, our approach was to reassure them that we were as interested in protecting Cambridge's heritage as they were. The College had nearly 800 years of common history with the City and our project was designed to see us through several centuries into the future. Equally, we were able to stress that we wanted to create something very different from the traditional image of Colleges, where high defensive exterior walls and limited access through narrow entrances guarded by Porters' Lodges give a sense of wanting to keep the City at bay. Pembroke's existing main College site was in fact one of very few which welcomed visitors. We argued that we wanted this new, major development to be even more outward looking, with easy access and open lines of sight into its gardens and buildings. Moreover, by the sensitive adaption of the United Reformed Church into an auditorium and the creation of an exhibition area above the new Trumpington Street entrance, we were looking to provide important spaces that could be used just as much by the City as the College.

Although frustrating in other ways, the delays caused by the University's internal decision-making gave the project team time to hone the details of the design. This in turn allowed

The Ferguson-Nazareth Room in Milstein House. It will be a reading room and a venue for intimate meetings and concerts. It was originally the grand Board Room of Stuart House when it was first built.

them better understand and engage with the very detailed heritage issues raised. There were some discussions which descended almost into a brick-by-brick debate, and the team needed to work at this level of knowledge. Our position was helped by an excellent heritage assessment carried out by Beacon (now Turley) Planning. Even more important, however, were the designs developed by our architects, Haworth Tompkins – and in particular the exceptional work of Beatie Blakemore. Her professional skills, detailed preparation, intelligent understanding and polite, dogged persistence convinced the planners on almost all of the contentious issues. Arguments were won not only on how we would adapt many of the existing buildings, but also on the demolition of 75 Trumpington Street, those jumbled additions to the back of Kenmare House and 6 Mill Lane, the Bailey, Grundy, Barrett Building and, most important of all, the huge edifice of the University Lecture Block. Although the frontage of Millers Yard remains as a reminder that not all arguments were won, at the end of a long, detailed process Council officials had been convinced on almost everything we wanted to do.

It also helped that we were able to work successfully in parallel with Historic England through their regional office. Their final report of 2019 found that:

> The new build elements of the proposals are potentially a major addition to the distinguished group of buildings that make up Pembroke College, and should enrich the conservation area while respecting its character and grain.

> Although some buildings will be lost, most notably the Lecture Rooms block, we have considered the justification provided, and the evidence of the options explored for potential retention, and believe that a convincing case has been made for their removal.

Similarly, our wide-ranging contacts with the local community, heritage groups, Ward Councillors and others all generated positive feedback. So with the scene set and momentum with us, all that remained was to receive the agreement of the City Council's Planning Committee. This they gave unanimously. Perhaps a little surprisingly, the only substantive points raised concerned the side issue of the planned pedestrian crossing on Trumpington Street.

6 The Mill Lane Gardens

Kurosh Davis

THE NEW GARDENS AND COURTYARDS continue the theme of College courtyards and gardens surrounded by inward-facing buildings which join at the corners.

CHIU COURT
The existing Porters' Lodge is linked by a new crossing that leads to the new part of the College. Passing through the arched Gatehouse, you arrive at the first courtyard: Chiu Court. This is largely paved and is a simple architectural space, in contrast to Dolby Court. A flexible gathering area, it is also a thoroughfare with seating and space for spill-out from the Church foyer.

At the heart of the courtyard, to one side of the main route we have made a more settled and contemplative space composed of two stone benches and a *Catalpa* tree. Here we have been able to collaborate with Alison Turnbull to create an ensemble of art and landscape that will encourage people to linger, think and question. We worked closely with Alison to convert her drawings

Planting in front of Dolby Court's west range: Viburnum cinnamomifolium, Hydrangea quercifolia, Carex *'Kyoto' and* Choisya *'Aztec Pearl'.*

Alison Turnbull's artwork in Chu Court includes a small basin in the stone bench. It trickles water into a channel leading through the mosaic in the centre.

and mock-ups into digital information that could be used to build the work to very tight tolerances.

The outer part of the work is formed by a Voronoi pattern of cut York stone. The result is like an exact mathematical version of a giraffe skin, derived from connecting lines that are equidistant between points in space. Within the frame of the stone benches is a tiled area that suggests another story, another space within a space. The mosaic tiles reflect Waterhouse's drawings for the College Library, now held in the College's archives. A bowl sits at the side of one of the benches; water emerges, spills down onto another bowl in the paving and trickles across the centre of the mosaic in a very narrow bronze channel. Standing here it is possible to see two related paintings in the interior of the foyer, suggesting a conversation between them and between the interior and exterior. The courtyard thus becomes a space of interactions, conversations and questions.

The planting around the courtyard continues a College tradition of using the rare and exotic. The *Catalpa* or Indian Bean tree, from the southeast of the United States, sets the scene with its showy panicles of white flowers in summer and large, heart-shaped leaves. *Melianthus major*, on the other hand, is native to South Africa and possesses distinctive large, blue-grey foliage. *Holboellia brachyandra*, an attractive evergreen climber from the understorey of Chinese forests, produces intriguing colourful flowers and fruits. Mediterranean plants are represented by a fig, *Bupleurum fruticosum*, and *Phlomis italica*, the Italian Jerusalem sage, as well as *Veronica peduncularis* 'Georgia Blue'. Other plants include *Veronica catarractae* from New Zealand, the Japanese aralia *Fatsia polycarpa* 'Green Fingers', which has beautiful, hand-shaped leaves, and, in another corner of the garden, a tree peony, *Paeonia* 'Black Pirate'. This last, notoriously difficult to propagate, produces dramatic deep-mahogany-red flowers in May.

BLYTH COURT

Next in the series of spaces is Blyth Court, a courtyard north of Milstein House facing onto Mill Lane. An avenue of pollarded lime trees frames the principal facade of the 1930s Classical Revival building and leads to an ornate iron screen and gates from the same period. Exotic climbers soften the courtyard and scale the walls to the east and west, among them Star Jasmine, Henry's Virginia creeper and climbing hydrangea. On one side the Rice Paper Plant, *Tetrapanax papyrifer* 'Rex', native to Taiwan, will provide an exotic flourish. And leaning into the facade of Milstein House will be an Antony Gormley sculpture, *Close*, generously loaned by the artist, as if seeking shelter within.

THE RAY AND DAGMAR DOLBY COURT

This Court is the largest space in the sequence. It is the greenest court, in the tradition of New Court. Both the edges of the space and the facades of the new buildings are heavily planted.

On the south side, wisteria cover the first two storeys, climbing up the columns of the arcaded walk.

The exotic Catalpa *or Indian Bean Tree in the heart of Chiu Court.*

Hydrangea quercifolia *in Chiu Court displaying the white flowers of early season.*

Below *Hydrangea quercifolia in Chiu Court. Its flowers gradually turn pink as the summer progresses.*

Above *The distinctive blue-grey foliage of* Melianthus major *in Chiu Court.*

Right *Planting in front of Dolby Court's south range:* Schizophragma integrifolium *'Windmills',* Carex *'Kyoto',* Boehmeria platanifolia *and* Choisya *'Aztec Pearl'.*

In front of this, the north side of the central lawn has an area of ornamental planting, including several medium-sized trees. On the east side a multi-stemmed Chinese scholar tree, *Styphnolobium japonicum*, anchors the east side of the space with its associations with temples, shrines and other sacred places. American Yellowwood, *Cladrastis kentukea*, is also grown here for its fine form, attractive compound leaves and fragrant, wisteria-like flowers. A Judas tree, *Cercis siliquastrum*, provides spring flowers. The smoke trees, *Cotinus coggygria*, are named after their inflorescences, which resemble a smoky haze or cloud in early summer. All these trees are tolerant of heat and drought.

Under the trees, ornamental planting encloses a series of seating spaces. The plants growing there, including oregano, lavenders, Russian sage, pale-purple coneflowers, blue stars and lilies, are adapted to the increasing heat of Cambridge summers. They are also good for pollinating insects.

Many of the plants in Dolby Court are evergreens or semi-evergreen and thus provide a welcome presence in winter. The evergreens include the Mexican *Choisya x dewitteana* 'Aztec Pearl', *Hedera colchica* 'Fall Favourite' and the wheel tree, *Trochodendron aralioides*, considered a sacred tree in Japan. A Chinese *Holboellia* or sausage vine, *Holboellia latifolia*, grows up the shadier walls. It will be interesting to see whether the warming summers and protected microclimate allow the *Holboellia* to develop its characteristic sausage-shaped fruits.

The central lawn, with its steps on the east side and banks on three sides, is designed as an outdoor carpet. It offers an informal meeting place to gather and sit.

7 The Environmental Sustainability of the Mill Lane Site

Joel Gustafsson

THE ENVIRONMENTAL IMPACT OF BUILDINGS

Buildings impact the environment in many ways, most of which impacts are commonly understood – the carbon emissions associated with energy used to heat cool, light and ventilate buildings, where the water comes from and the materials used to construct them. Others are less tangible or obvious, for instance the upfront investment required to ensure that the buildings can be adapted and altered by future generations and are resilient to climate change.

There are a range of guidance documents, certification schemes, target performance metrics and case studies that offer a view of environmental sustainability within buildings. Each has its merits and issues, and there are many differences between them.

The Mill Lane project was delivered in two phases, but consists of (at least) seven projects, which differ according to use, age, heritage significance or the extent of new build versus refurbishment. In terms of environmental sustainability, the repurposing of the United Reformed Church is a completely different challenge to the construction of Dolby Court, for example.

A redevelopment of this scale offered the opportunity to consider each of the environmental impacts and make specific briefing and design decisions that minimise the impact to the environment, at both a local and global scale. This opportunity has been seized.

ABANDONING GAS

The production of heat is the main energy demand for UK buildings. When the design stage of the Mill Lane project commenced in 2017, it was orthodox to use natural gas for this purpose. Indeed, 'gas' and 'heat' remain synonymous for many. One of the most progressive decisions was to abandon gas. This was considered brave, risky and perhaps even foolhardy by some. However, the direction of both UK and global energy in the

Opposite *The network of pipes behind the air-source heat pump system for the whole Mill Lane site.*

Far left *Under-concrete work in progress. Reinforcing steel bars have been added to the concrete for strength and the red pipework runs to chilled soffits, ensuring the best cooling effect for student rooms in Dolby Court in summer.*

Left *The facades of the new ranges of Dolby Court have been designed in traditional brick and stone, and the windows are deeply shaded.*

subsequent years has shown this to be a sensible and pragmatic judgement.

We spend most of our time in buildings. For those who work indoors, this can be almost 24 hours a day, particularly during winter. Over the course of the twentieth century our expectations of comfort have increased. It is thus easy to see why almost one-quarter of the UK's carbon emissions are directly attributed to the heating of buildings.

Energy transitions are not simple, but they are also not new. At Pembroke College's foundation in the fourteenth century, heat was derived from wood and peat, both of which are challenging to harvest, dry, transport and store. Heat was thus a luxury rather than the expectation it has become today. Coal was transformative: it was energy-dense and the pace of the Industrial Revolution (and its associated technology) made it cheap and plentiful. Looking at the roofscape of Pembroke College and the wider city, we can see the way in which the buildings were altered and adapted to make use of this in the pursuit of warmth.

The impact on air quality is difficult for the twenty-first-century reader to comprehend. Consider the sensation in your throat and eyes caused by each chimney with a raging coal fire at its base on a cold, still, winter morning. The discomfort, respiratory diseases and nuisance this produced was justified by the reduction in illness and death, the consequences of living in cold and damp buildings.

Gas, by comparison, is extremely 'clean'. The nitrogen oxide$_x$ gases produced by burning it are problematic, but nothing compared to the smog from coal fires. Gas was quite literally a life saver by comparison. It also comes in pipes. The need for deliveries, storage and dealing with ash are all gone, along with the improvement in pipework and radiators that move heat from fuel to room.

A Twenty-First-Century Energy Transition

Past energy transitions have arisen because they offered improvements in both amenity and efficiency: we could have more for less. The

Dolby Court facing Mill Lane. The planning permission required the previous Miller's Yard frontage to be maintained, and the new buildings to be tied in with it.

technological developments that followed the availability of fuels increased our ability to use them. The comfortable environments that we provide would be unrecognisable to the first occupants of our existing buildings, including those from the relatively recent past. Alterations, sometimes brutal and ignorant, were embraced towards this aim.

The transition to electricity for heat is different – this time there is not an amenity incentive. Efficiency is important but invisible to most. So why should this take place?

In time gas will run out; the transition away from its use is an inevitable technical challenge. This is, of course, still some decades away. The motivation to consider alternatives comes from placing an intrinsic value on environmental impact. The burden of assessing the technical considerations, accepting the risks and delivering the precedents falls to those brave enough to do so. In this regard the Mill Lane project is leading by example.

The industrial heritage of the site is interesting and relevant. The Cambridge Electricity Supply Company was one of the first formed in the UK. Its headquarters sat within the Mill Lane site in the Bailey, Grundy, Barrett building. Bricks from its demolition have been reused in the small building housing the electrical transformers that enable the full electrification of the site – an outcome that Cambridge's electricity supply company was unlikely to have been able to foresee at the turn of the twentieth century.

What and How?

The Mill Lane site uses air-source heat pumps to supply all of the heating and domestic hot water needs of the site. The system uses low temperatures (45°C rather than the 75°C of traditional gas combustion central heating systems) to enable efficiencies of over 350 per cent. For each unit of electricity, 3.5 units of heat are provided.

There is nothing inherently innovative or new in this approach, other than the technical challenges of using low temperatures to warm old buildings. The Auditorium is perhaps the best example of this on the site. The building uses almost one-third of the whole site heat demand and needs underfloor heating, fan-assisted radiators, and a heater on the fresh air supply.

Delivering Innovation and Leading the Way

The surrounding air is the main heat source for the buildings; heat pumps use the air by cooling down large volumes of it. They are typically located on roofs or remote compounds, but neither was possible on the constrained Mill Lane site. The resultant approach to moving air described below is a first.

The heat is taken from the air in the yard between the University Centre and Dolby Court to the west of the site, directly below the windows of the students in the West Block. To keep down noise, the size of the fans is increased and the speed at which they run is reduced.

The large fans have an industrial appearance that is managed by moving them into the building. The heat pumps are effectively in a cave. Locating both the intake and discharge pumps on the same face of the building is without precedent.

To address this, a factory test of the heat exchangers was undertaken and alterations made to the facade. These changes mean that the heavier discharged air is not sucked back into the inlets. The operational data will show the efficacy of this approach and set a precedent that can be replicated for challenging urban sites. In so doing, it will reduce the hurdles for others seeking to embrace the energy transition of their buildings.

Renewable Generation

An all-electric design adds weight to the economic case for on-site solar photovoltaic (PV) panels, in addition to the strong environmental case. A decision was made to maximise the use of PV generation across the site; all roofs with good exposure to the sun have thus been used to accommodate PV panels. This should support about one-quarter of the site's annual electricity use and reduce the demand on the wider energy system.

LONGEVITY IN A CHANGING CLIMATE

The climate is changing – it is getting warmer, wetter and more erratic. In July 2019, Cambridge set the UK temperature record of 38.7 °C. Only three years later this was exceeded, with temperatures reaching 40.3 °C in Lincolnshire. Cambridge was not far behind, at 39.9 °C. According to most climate models, a lot of this warming increase is now 'baked in'. If we stopped emissions tomorrow, warming would still continue for several decades.

Water is equally as important an issue within Cambridge. The summer of 2022 saw a record drought for the water-stressed region. Shortly afterwards, the winter of 2023/24 saw record rainfall.

The north block of Dolby Court, where the windows face south, will receive direct sunlight during summer months. In order to cool the rooms inside the building, the windows have been heavily recessed and shaded.

The Foyer makes beautiful use of the stone wall of the former church, and reclaimed bricks from the site's old school hall.

Dolby Court's west range has a ventilation chimney echoing the historic chimneys of the College, and solar panels on the roof.

An adaptive response to these water challenges has been taken, complementing the measures to reduce carbon emissions and energy use.

Closing the Metabolism

The design of Dolby Court incorporates the tools of passive design to reduce the need for cooling. These include thermal mass, optimised window sizes and solar control of the glass, external shading within the window construction, plus generous and secure openings to ventilate at night. However, the inevitability of severe heatwaves is accepted and a low-energy cooling solution has also been incorporated.

Within Dolby Court, the concrete ceilings have pipes embedded in them. Cool water can be circulated through these to create a cold surface, like a church for a summer wedding. The heat is then pumped to the heat-pump system, where it is

Opposite An aerial view of Chiu Court, the Auditorium and the public-facing buildings of the Mill Lane site. The historic College and the rest of south Cambridge are visible beyond.

used to provide domestic hot water. The rooms are effectively a solar-heat collector, with the increased comfort a byproduct of running the showers.

Water

The landscape quality is as important to the project as the buildings. Planting decisions have been heavily influenced by drought resistance, but extreme events remain a challenge. Irrigation is needed during heatwaves to allow even the hardiest of plants to flourish rather than simply to survive.

Rainfall is captured from the roofs and stored in 13,000 litres of tanks below ground. During prolonged droughts, this will be used to keep the newly formed court vibrant. In such times, the water in the tanks will deplete but it can be topped up by an extraction borehole, 60m deep, installed in front of Milstein House. This means that no irrigation water will come from the city main nor the aquifer that serves it.

MATERIAL CHOICES

The most sustainable building materials are those that already exist. Carbon emissions associated with the production and transport of new materials are released into the atmosphere even at this critical moment, when the world's natural systems are being strained.

During the early stages of the project, the extent of demolition was extensively reviewed. Approximately half of the space provided is within retained and refurbished buildings. The embodied carbon of the materials is a 'sunk cost'; their upgrade and reuse avoids new emissions, waste generation and resource use.

The new buildings (Foyer, Gatehouse and Dolby Court) were carefully considered and their material impact carefully and accurately quantified. The result presented a tension. Timber has a lower embodied carbon impact than either concrete and steel, hence its use for the relatively simple Foyer and Gatehouse. However, Dolby Court is constructed from concrete. The reason lies in longevity – not of the material itself, as timber will last almost indefinitely provided that it is kept dry, but in the future use of the space.

The most cherished collegiate buildings have been used for centuries. During this time they have generally been altered and manipulated to suit the needs of successive generations. A concrete building allowed a readily adaptable form that could support a variety of alterations. However, the timber alternative required more columns and structural walls that would make alteration extremely complex, if not impossible.

WHAT DOES SUSTAINABILITY LOOK LIKE?

It would be arrogant to proclaim that this project is a beacon of sustainable development as it is completed. This can only be judged by those looking back from future decades.

The decisions that we have made and the completed project certainly meet our present needs. We have deliberately prioritised long-term sustainability at each decision point in the hope that we have also helped future generations.

As the buildings age, natural gas will run out and carbon dioxide concentrations will rise, and then (we hope) fall, taking temperatures with them. Cambridge will see extremes of heat, cold, rain and drought. Throughout this we have given the buildings every chance of remaining comfortable, adaptable, efficient and cherished, so that their sustainability is demonstrated through longevity and joy for many generations to come.

Part III
Study and Reflection

8 Pembroke's Gardens

Sarah Claydon and
Loraine Gelsthorpe

Pembroke Gardens possess an eclectic collection of plants that have just as much presence as the buildings. In many ways the collection reflects the whole personality and history of the College: interesting, mature, but with many pockets of innovation.

Several individuals have contributed to the unique character of the Gardens. Meredith Dewey was an architect for change during his time as Dean at Pembroke from 1936 to 1983. Alongside the Head Gardeners he looked to move away from municipality, instead bringing colour and a wide range of unexpected plants. Dewey was seen at College meetings looking through nursery catalogues, picking out the latest beautiful or unusual plant he wanted to introduce through his role as Garden Steward. As a new Fellow in 1936, he did away with two tulip beds and created a rockery along Ridley's Walk.

Dewey served in the Navy during the Second World War. He returned in 1946 to be told that he should extend the rockery, as the Chaplain, Wilfred Knox, had taken over the original rockery area. Following Knox's death in 1950, Dewey cared for the whole rockery, now filled with a myriad of alpines and dwarf conifers; he was often found working on the rockery in the afternoons.

The giant *Gunnera manicata*, next to the Hobson's Conduit-fed pond, was a remarkable feature along Ridley's Walk. The pond is still there, now surrounded by ferns and punctuated with stonework from long-gone structures. They remind us of an incident in which Dewey spied Fellow Ellis Minns furtively removing some of the stones that he had employed in the rockery structure. Given that these were part of the College's fourteenth-century Hall, Minns believed they deserved a more distinguished resting place than as part of a rockery wall. Sadly the *Gunnera manicata* (known colloquially as 'giant rhubarb') is no more.

Today one of the highlights along Ridley's Walk is an enormous *Musa basjoo*. Known as

Ridley's Walk, alongside the Junior Parlour, passes along a border full of flowers.

The entrance to the Master's Lodge. In the early summer, the arbour is awash with roses.

The Avenue, looking towards the Chapel; John Farnham's Crescent Figure *sculpture is just beyond the gates.*

the Japanese banana or hardy banana, the plant clearly enjoyed the extreme heat in the summer of 2022, when it produced four flowers. The wet autumn that followed, and temperatures of -12°C in the winter of 2022, did it no favours, however, leaving the College to wait with bated breath in the spring of 2023 to see whether the plant had survived. Fortunately its sheltered position and, perhaps, the hot-water pipe running under the nearby path ensured its survival. By the end of summer one would hardly have known that in May the *Musa basjoo* had been reduced to ground level, the marvellous *Trachycarpus fortunei* filling in until it was once again reduced to a background feature.

Dewey was heard to say that 'the truth about the Gardens Committee is that they just don't like flowers'. This may explain why two current members of the committee – who joined it in the late 1990s and early 2000s under the watchful eye of the Chair, Bill Grimstone – were each given a plant to care for in a pot. They were also asked to identify plants and to care for a small patch, as one would give a child to tend. When Brian Watchorn became Gardens Committee Chair, they were then tasked with managing larger areas of the garden and planning planting for the changing seasons, keeping colour and scent firmly in mind. The JP bed, Orchard bed and Winter bed have all developed distinctive characters from the personal interest of Fellows on the Gardens Committee. Also, to be fair, today's Committee are passionate about flowers!

A TIME OF CHANGE

In 2020, ordinary life in the College was interrupted by the Covid-19 pandemic. The grounds grew quiet and the solitary figure of Senior Gardener Sebastian Filipek was seen

The northwest corner of New Court, built in 1881–2 by George Gilbert Scott Jr.

working the main site and hostels, usually tended by four full-time and one part-time member of staff. The Head Porter, Gordon Murray, was even seen mowing Old Court as everyone helped each other out. In early 2021, Nick Firman decided it was time to hang up his trowel after 56 years of service, 53 of them as Head Gardener.

Sarah Claydon came in as Head Gardener in August 2021, and wasted no time in getting the College ready for the winter planting. Come springtime something new was clearly happening, as thousands of bulbs popped up all over the place. In the summer the traditional rows of bedding plants in Old Court and Ivy Court, in particular, were significantly reduced in number. A push towards sustainability means that there are fewer bedding plants but more perennial plants. More recently, areas have been set aside for 're-wilding', for example behind the Henry Moore sculpture on Foundress Court lawn, where a new wildflower meadow is under development, and part of the Master's Garden at the front of the Lodge. Nor is the Orchard mown down so quickly as before, allowing wildflower seed, distributed from bales collected from the new King's College Hay Meadow, to start taking hold. This year in particular has yielded colourful displays of dark-red hyacinths, alongside daffodils and crocuses – all bulbs relocated from previous spring displays elsewhere.

Feijoa sellowiana flourishes in the historic gardens of the College.

Ivy Court (1614–70) has also undergone considerable transformation. Colourful, year-round pots in the centre draw attention to the wonderful sculpture (*Natural Pearl*) on loan from artist Nigel Hall RA. The steps and ramp leading to the screens outside the Dining Hall were softened with pots of *Fatsia* over the years. Recently they have been replaced by large wooden planters filled with *Salvia cerro potosi*, *Pittosporum illicioides var angustifolium*, *Erigeron karvinskianus* 'Lavender Lady', *Calamintha nepeta* 'Blue Cloud', *Carex Testacea* and a *Toona sinensis* 'Flamingo' to enhance the court further.

FRUITS OF THE GARDENS

For many years the Orchard has been the centre of the spring bulb display at the College. As summer draws on, however, the fruit trees start to produce their bounties. Quinces have recently been used in gin and preserves, while mulberries feature in sauces and in desserts at events. Apples from the various College hostels are either available for all to help themselves to or used in desserts. The multi-fruited family apple tree (donated by a Fellow to reflect her 20-year milestone of working at the College) normally produces sufficient apples for a Sunday evening apple pie on High Table.

Figs have also recently been used in salads and chutneys. The medlars, a fruit that attracts a lot of comment, have to be picked in the autumn before the first frosts, then left to 'blet'. This process of 'managed rotting' softens the fruit, allowing the Catering department of the College to make a jelly usually served with cheese. Throughout the year catering staff use the new herb garden, by the greenhouse at the end of the Avenue, to gather ingredients for dishes.

As planting is reviewed throughout the College, increasing numbers of edible plants are being added. These range from well-known herbs to tomatoes, and plants that evoke the reaction 'I didn't know you could eat that'. The edible side of the garden is important to the current Gardens team. For the Catering department, it can help to reduce food miles, and in using seasonal produce and creating perceptions in diners' minds of Pembroke's gardens as a working and productive place. For the College members, it not only reduces the reliance on supermarket pots of herbs but also, more importantly, fosters a sense that these gardens are there for them to use; it is their home.

Old Court was briefly transformed between 1983 and 2004 by a walnut tree, planted to commemorate 20 years since the election of Ian Fleming, David Hussain and John Waldram to the Fellowship. Unfortunately the juglone secretions from the tree meant that the lawn suffered and so, after 20 years, the tree was removed. Today a small divot marks the spot where the tree grew, causing Gardeners to mutter as the lawnmower is thrown off course during mowing. Old Court has limited space for planting, but that has not stopped the Gardens team from filling it with photo-worthy plants. The *Billardiera heterophylla*, *Stauntonia hexaphylla* and *Muehlenbeckia complexa* are the latest additions to provide height and interest to the narrowest border, found outside

Wisteria beside the Library provides beautiful flowers and fragrance in late spring.

the Old Library and the Catering department. The planting aims to have year-round interest. During the summers to date, this has included salvias, dahlias, *Verbena bonariensis*, *Cineraria* and a few of the traditional standard fuchsias and heliotropes. In winter heuchera, *Bellis perennis*, cineraria and a large number of hyacinths and tulips have so far been used.

NEW GARDEN SPACES

Following the building of Foundress Court, four garden spaces were created. The Nihon Garden, bounded by the new subterranean car park, Tennis Court Road and the Nihon Room, is a restful, Japanese-style garden. By all accounts, the gardeners at the time were not specialists in the Japanese style; they therefore sought assistance from the Japanese Garden Society who were able to come and support the maintenance. In March 2022, the enforced neglect caused by the Covid-19 pandemic was evident. Five bulk bags of pruning soon brought it back to shape, however, and it is once again an urban retreat. The garden entrance (from the underground car park) now includes a bamboo screen, and a chestnut, Japanese-style gateway, which cleverly conceals the car park from within, but is inviting from the outside.

The roof garden (the raised bed in the Nihon Building) has undergone two major facelifts in its brief history. The first iteration included large white stones, reminiscent of the Japanese gravel gardens, but these soon became green with algae. It was suggested (tongue in cheek) that cleaning the stones could be used to help bring wayward students back into line – a 'green' form of community service! Eventually one bed with a bamboo and another with box hedging alongside shortened railway sleepers gave way to a Japanese-inspired replanting. Large containers were scorched to imitate the Japanese *shou sugi ban* method of burning wood to preserve it. The new planters and the two existing beds are now filled with planting that uses greens, leaf shape and movement to create a peaceful space. This can be viewed and enjoyed from the corridors that surround the space.

Once Foundress Court had been built, an extra path was needed to link the Junior Parlour and the new building. The new plan allowed for the creation of new patio areas, along with seating, enclosed by yew hedging. The rest of the Bowling Green was surrounded by box hedging to the north and east.

CHALLENGES FOR THE GARDENS

Like every team before them, the gardeners have to battle or manage the latest pests or diseases. The most recent is the double threat to the *Buxus sempervirens* (box) hedging. Box blight is sweeping across the country, but thankfully we have not seen this yet. On the other hand the box tree moth, *Cydalima perspectalis*, has been munching through the box hedges around the Bowling Green. The hedging has gone brown in areas heavily damaged by the moths. There has been great relief that the College does not have any large topiary that we would feel compelled to save. Instead we have weighed up all options and made a decision to remove all the box hedging. The plan is to use a variety of species so that each distinct area is replanted with different species. This will, hopefully, reduce the impact of future pests and outbreaks of disease.

With dying box hedges and increasing awareness of the environment and sustainability, one recent initiative includes the creation of a dead hedge. Students and gardeners built the 'hedge' together, in the corner of the footpath

Above *The Virginia creeper draped over the archway behind the Orchard turns a glorious red each autumn.*

Left *A line of London Plane trees, some leaning significantly, adorns the Avenue. Foundress Court, visible behind, was built in 1997, long after the trees were established.*

Right *The borders along Ridley's Walk are famous for their beauty. The planting includes* Cleome hasslerianna *with* Cosmos bipinnatus *'Dazzler' (back) and* Persicaria orientalis *'Cerise Pearls' (front).*

Below *This magnificent planting scheme in Ivy Court features* Aster frikartii *and* Sesleria autumnalis *(front) with* Scabiosa columbaria, Cosmos bipinnatus *'Dazzler'*, Perovskia *'Blue Spire'*, Origanum laevigatum *'Herrenhausen' and* Alium shaerocephalon.

leading from the Avenue to the Junior Parlour, then infilled it with plants. These will link the naturalistic orchard with the formal Bowling Green. A mixture of native plants and cultivated versions, including *Deschampsia cespitosa* 'Goldtau', *Sanguisorba officinalis* 'Red Thunder', *Ranunculus acris*, Cow Parsley and Feverfew, will help to tie everything together.

We should also mention here the Avenue adorned by London Planes, some of which lean quite dramatically. However, they are regularly checked by Arboriculturalists. We have also had PiCUS tests and climbing inspections done to check the health of the trees, which fortunately are still going strong.

HAVENS OF PEACE

On the opposite side of the avenue, an arboretum of trees, including the wonderfully named *Acer pseudoplatanus* 'Brilliantissimum' (which sounds like something out of a Harry Potter novel), has been lifted with an underplanting of spring bulbs that die back in time for the summer events. In summer months the Avenue becomes a good area to play boules and petanque. The adjacent Fellows' Garden can almost feel like an after-thought, with its mature shrubs and trees.

The *Calocedrus decurrens*, or 'Incense Cedar', is one of the last vestiges of the large Master's pleasure Garden. It was linked to the 1933 Master's Lodge, demolished to make way for Foundress Court. A shady garden, the addition of *Thalictrum tuberiferum*, Digitalis and *Leycesteria formosa* 'Purple Rain', among other plants, has helped to lift the area, ahead of full renovation plans. The summerhouse remains a welcome retreat for members of the Fellows' Gardens Committee when walking the grounds on wet days; it is also a cooling stop in summer.

Library Lawn was the original Master's Garden until the 1870s. The intricately laid out beds and mature trees, seen in David Loggan's engraving of 1690 (p. 16), have now given way to a large lawn – a favourite venue for social functions and matriculation and sports team photographs. At the Chapel end the *Rosa* 'La Sevillana', underplanted with *Nepeta* 'Six Hills Giant', are show stoppers until the first frosts. Pitt sits among a renovated shady border with a 'woodland feel'. Seating in front of the Hitcham building and on the relatively new patio area are favoured areas – for students and Fellows alike – to bask in the sun and ponder a visit to the library opposite.

Pembroke's gardens are distinct yet flow naturally into one another. They feature both formal and informal areas, but above all they are warm and welcoming.

9 The Old Library

Stephen Halliday

The building now known as the Old Library has led a long, eventful and occasionally hazardous life. It escaped an act of shameless vandalism in the seventeenth century and survived a death sentence pronounced by the Fellowship in the nineteenth century, passed on the advice of an eminent Victorian architect.

THE FIRST COLLEGE CHAPEL

It was the practice of the early medieval Colleges for members to worship in nearby churches, in Pembroke's case St Botolph's. However, in 1355 the Foundress obtained a licence from Pope Innocent VI for Pembroke to have its own chapel. It appears that little progress was made in building this, since in 1366 a fresh licence was granted by his successor, Pope Urban V. No records about the construction work that followed are available, but we do know that by 1398 the Bishop of Ely licensed the celebration of Mass, so it had evidently been completed by that date. This makes Pembroke's Chapel the

Above *A photograph of Old Court before Alfred Waterhouse demolished the left-side range in 1874; the Old Library is on the far right.*

Opposite *The Old Library, built as the College Chapel in 1385, was converted into a library in 1690. It is now a venue for meetings and dinners.*

University's oldest building still in use by its original owner, with the single exception of the Dining Hall of Peterhouse. There was also a chaplain's residence on E staircase in the vicinity of the room now known as the Christopher Smart Room.

Our knowledge of this Chapel is dependent upon David Loggan's 1690 engraving of the College (p. 16), which shows a Gothic west window with five lights and a bell tower. The material used was probably clunch, a chalky limestone rock much used in East Anglia. Bricks would not have been readily available at this time as the art of brickmaking, brought to England by the Romans, had been taken home with them when the Legions left in AD 410. It would not be rediscovered and in widespread use again until the fifteenth century.

AN ICONOCLAST WHO ENJOYED HIS WORK

By the time of Loggan's engraving, the internal features of the Chapel had been vandalised by William Dowsing on the orders of Parliament. In 1643, as civil war was waged between the forces of Charles I and those of Parliament, Dowsing was sent to East Anglia with a Parliamentary Commission to destroy 'all Monuments of Superstition and Idolatry'. He clearly enjoyed his work, writing a gleeful account of the trail of destruction that marked his passage. In December Dowsing went to King's College and announced that he was going to celebrate Christmas by destroying the windows of the Chapel, the finest surviving examples of the glazier's art. They had outlasted the earlier iconoclasm of Thomas Cromwell because they had been installed at the expense of his master, Henry VIII. Fortunately, much of the Parliamentarian army was quartered in the Chapel over the winter. Cromwell's general told Dowsing, no doubt in soldierly language, that the prospect of spending the winter in a windowless building was not attractive and that Dowsing should be on his way.

Dowsing then turned his attention to Pembroke, which had earlier, and unwisely, attempted to send most of its silverware to the King in York to support him in his campaign against Parliament. The gesture was futile since the silver was intercepted by Cromwell's forces and passed into the hands of the Parliamentarian faction, but it meant that Pembroke was branded as disloyal to Parliament. Armed both with this knowledge and his Commission, Dowsing descended upon the College, probably on Boxing Day 1643. After overcoming some strenuous verbal resistance from the Fellows, he recorded that he 'broak 10 cherubims. We broak and

Left *Pembroke's Chapel, built by Christopher Wren in 1665, enabled the former chapel to become the Old Library. The Chapel was extended by George Gilbert Scott Jr in 1881.*

Above Henry Doogood's Old Library ceiling, created in 1690.

Below Bishop Matthew Wren, Bishop of Ely, President of Pembroke (and Master of Peterhouse), commissioned Pembroke's new Chapel. The building was completed in 1665.

pulled down 80 superstitious pictures'. These were presumably the stained-glass windows.

The Chapel, now in a ruined state, appears to have remained in use until the new Chapel, by Christopher Wren, was consecrated in 1665. The work was paid for by the young man's uncle, Matthew Wren, after his release from the Tower of London, where he had been confined by order of Parliament for 18 years. Matthew was at the time President of Pembroke and Bishop of Ely. The only remnant of the original Chapel is its piscina, a stone basin once used for washing vessels used in the Mass. This piscina is now set into the south wall of the chancel of the Wren Chapel.

In 1690 the former chapel was thoroughly refurbished and turned into a Library, with a ceiling by Henry Doogood. The finest plasterer of his age, Doogood had worked on many of Sir Christopher Wren's London churches. His long association with Wren has led to the assumption that the overall design of the new Library was that of Wren himself, compounded by the fact that Wren's brother-in-law was a Fellow of the College at the time (and paid for much of the work), while Wren's son was a Fellow Commoner at Pembroke. The ceiling is one of Doogood's finest. It incorporates the date 1690; the Royal coat of arms of William and Mary and that of the Foundress; books; representations of the four 'elements' of earth, water, air and fire; foliage; hunting scenes and birds in flight as seen from below. The woodwork is also of the highest quality. One pair of bookcases was left in place, with its contents, when the new Library was built by Waterhouse in the 1870s; the other bookcase ends were set into the walls, showing the intricate carvings of grotesque masks and naturalistic friezes. The carving was probably done by the local firm of Cornelius Austin, who had also done the carving for the Wren Chapel. At about the same time the north wall of the building, facing Pembroke Street, was faced with brick. The south wall, facing Old Court, was faced with Ketton limestone in the eighteenth century, at the same time as much of Old Court.

A NEW THREAT

The Old Library, having emerged proudly from the depredations of William Dowsing, thus faced a greater threat almost two centuries later from a distinguished Victorian architect. In 1870, as the University experienced a rapid growth in the number of students, the 42-year Mastership of Gilbert Ainslie came to an end. He was succeeded by John Power, whose ten years in office witnessed a transformation in the size and appearance of Pembroke, the number of undergraduates almost tripling during his Mastership from 43 to 122. The eminent architect Alfred Waterhouse, best known for his work on the Natural History Museum in Kensington, was invited by the Fellows to suggest 'the best way of providing for the college a group of buildings as efficient, convenient and architecturally effective as the site was capable of'.

Above *Details of the Old Library plasterwork by Henry Doogood, 1690. The designs represent a hunting scene (top left), the Royal coat of arms (top right) and a cherub.*

Left *The Old Library. Two original bookcases were preserved, with the Royal coat of arms behind, when the Library moved out in 1878.*

Overleaf *Old Court, with the Dining Hall on the right and the Old Library on the left; the range facing us dates from the late fourteenth century.*

The Old Library and the Porters' Lodge, with the tower of the University's Pitt Building behind.

Waterhouse was probably chosen because of his espousal of the 'Victorian Gothic' style, in keeping with Pembroke's medieval origins and buildings. He began well with the new residential quarter of Red Buildings and the present Library, with its Continental Gothic character and Belgian-style clocktower. When he proposed demolishing the Dining Hall, however, his plans began to cause misgivings among the Fellows, provoking a lively correspondence from alumni who included churchmen, headmasters and academics. Despite this the Dining Hall was demolished – but when Waterhouse then suggested the demolition of both the Wren Chapel and the Old Library the Fellows rallied, as recorded in the diaries of John Neville Keynes (father of the economist Maynard Keynes). They decided instead to appoint an architect 'whose style is specially conservative' – a verdict that offended Waterhouse, who regarded himself as falling into that category.

A DEATH SENTENCE

Nevertheless, the Fellows had voted, in 1878, to demolish the now redundant Old Library. George Gilbert Scott Jr (son of Sir George and father of Sir Giles), the newly appointed architect, inherited this verdict. Scott was noted for his cautious approach to conservation and he did nothing to execute the Fellows' earlier decision to demolish the building. He is remembered for designing New Court, but should also be remembered for saving the Old Library, observing to the Fellows that 'I have no doubt at all that what remains of the ancient buildings of the College should be religiously preserved'. On 26 April 1880 he wrote, with specific reference to the Old Library, 'I do not wish to have the discredit of having destroyed a

The principal door to the Old Library. The key is a huge one, and very heavy.

fine old room'. The Fellows duly voted to rescind the earlier decision to destroy the building and to refurbish it instead.

Today the room is used for meetings, lectures, examinations and other College activities. In 2014 the Old Library was filled with scaffolding to carry out a major refurbishment of this Grade I-listed edifice. The plaster was thoroughly cleaned and repaired, and a new heating and air-conditioning system was installed. The listed status of the building necessitated the installation of the chiller unit for the air conditioning in a pit in the northwest corner of Ivy Court, at the foot of the steps leading down from the screens.

Sadly, the many visitors who come to the College rarely see the splendours of the Old Library because it is in use for much of the time. However, they do not have to go far to see Doogood's work. Next door to Marks & Spencer, Market Hill has a first-floor room visible from the pavement whose ceiling, on a smaller scale, has many of the features of the Old Library. Presumably Doogood did it on his day off. And for cash in hand!

10 Ridley's Walk: A Protestant Martyr, an Orchard, a Banana and Two Inventors

Stephen Halliday

Stephen Halliday came up to Pembroke in 1961 to read history, graduating in 1964. In 2006 he retired and moved back to Cambridge, where he qualified as a Cambridge Blue Badge Guide. He learned that Pembroke welcomes more tour groups than any College but King's. He also observed that many visitors comment that one always sees students in Pembroke, with its paths and small, friendly courtyards, whereas they are a rare sight in the larger spaces of King's, Trinity and St John's. Pembroke, they think, looks and feels more like a home than a stately home. One of the byways of the College that makes the strongest impression on visitors is Ridley's Walk, of which Stephen has written the following account.

RIDLEY'S WALK
Ridley's Walk runs from the east end of Ivy Court (long since divested of its ivy), alongside M and N staircases, to its junction with New Court. It bears the name of the Protestant martyr Nicholas

A portrait of Nicholas Ridley, Fellow of Pembroke from 1524 and Master from 1540–53, by an unknown artist. Ridley was also Bishop of Rochester and then of London. He was burned at the stake in Oxford by Queen Mary in 1555 and became a celebrated Protestant martyr.

The Archway from Ivy Court to the Orchard, as seen from the Orchard. This is the start of Ridley's Walk.

Ridley, who in 1555 remembered it in the moments before his death at the stake in Oxford. Ridley came to Pembroke in 1518, became a fellow in 1524 and was Master from 1540–53. He welcomed Henry VIII's break with Rome, became a king's chaplain and successively Bishop of Rochester and London while remaining Master.

In July 1553, as Edward VI, the 15-year-old heir and only son of Henry VIII, lay dying, he named his cousin Lady Jane Grey as his successor, to ensure a Protestant succession. Ridley signed the Letters Patent to the Privy Council to confirm her as Queen. Three days later, on 9 July 1553, for good measure, Ridley declared at St Paul's that Henry VIII's two daughters, the Princesses Mary and Elizabeth, were 'Bastards'. This proved unwise. Within nine days Mary had become Queen and Ridley was removed to the Tower of London. The new Catholic monarch set about purging England of its Protestant bishops. Ridley, together with Hugh Latimer (Clare College, Bishop of Winchester) and Thomas Cranmer (Jesus College, Archbishop of Canterbury), was gaoled in Oxford in March 1554. Following a brief trial, Ridley and Latimer were burned at the stake on

16 October 1555 on a site now marked by a cross in Oxford's Broad Street. Cranmer, soon to follow them, was compelled to watch. As he awaited his fate, bound to the stake, Ridley's final thoughts were of his College, as recorded in *Foxe's Book of Martyrs* (1563):

> Farewell Pembroke Hall, of late my own Colledge, my Cure and my charge ... In thy Orchard (the walls, buts and trees, if they could speak, would bear me witnesse), I Learned without booke [i.e. by heart] all Paul's Epistles, yea and all the Canonical Epistles, save only the Apocalypse...

He ended by wishing that 'All the holy scripture may ever abide in that Colledge so long as the World shall endure'.

On 16 October each year Ridley is venerated in the calendar of saints. In 1928 the widow of W.H. Ridley, a descendant of the martyred bishop, bequeathed to Pembroke a rare family heirloom: a handsome Tudor chair. The 'Ridley Chair' now resides in the Chapel. The Master sits in it when welcoming new Fellows and matriculating students to the College.

THE ORCHARD

Ridley's Walk contains many memorable features, more often noticed by visitors to the College than by its residents. To the right, as we enter from Ivy Court, opposite the Graduate Parlour, is the site of the original orchard that Ridley recalled. It is now a wild garden containing a variety of flowers, shrubs and trees. Conspicuous among them is a mulberry tree on its mound. This tree is descended from one of a collection of mulberries imported by James I in a vain attempt to promote the growth of an English silk industry. Unfortunately it proved to be the wrong kind of mulberry for that purpose, but it does produce a modest crop of mulberries for jelly – which, with the agreement of Head Gardener Sarah Claydon, is harvested by the head of Catering Nina Rhodes and used to make a compote to be served with duck. Nina also takes the fruit from the medlar tree to make a very sweet jelly for High Table.

In front of the wild garden and adjacent to the path are the remains of the rock garden. This was the particular preserve of the Dean, the Reverend Meredith Dewey. It became the home of the rare plants that he collected on his numerous foreign trips and brought into the country in the protective custody of his sandwiches.

Reverend Meredith Dewey, from 1936–83, Dean of Pembroke and enhancer of the College gardens.

Ridley's Walk and Pembroke's 'banana tree', in fact a giant herb, beside the entrance to the Junior Parlour.

A GIANT HERB

Further along on the left of the path, near the entrance to N staircase, grows a plant that is botanically a giant herb but is better known as Pembroke's 'banana'. It has been there for almost 20 years. Its imminent demise was often confidently predicted as winter approached, but it was protected against frosts in its early years by an enveloping shroud, placed on it by Pembroke's long-serving Head Gardener Nick Firman. The plant has long outgrown its protector and has acclimatised to its sheltered corner of the gardens. It makes a strong impression on visitors, but is scarcely noticed by the students who pass it daily on their way to and from the Junior Parlour.

Ridley's Walk from the Orchard; the loveliest border in the College gardens is on the left.

Ridley's Walk, surrounded by flowers, leads in the direction of the Orchard Building, which dates from 1957.

10 RIDLEY'S WALK: A PROTESTANT MARTYR, AN ORCHARD, A BANANA AND TWO INVENTORS

The commemorative plaque for Sir Harold Ridley, pioneer of cataract surgery.

SIR HAROLD RIDLEY

At the end of Ridley's Walk, where it joins New Court, is a low wall. On this is mounted a blue plaque honouring one of Nicholas Ridley's descendants. It reads:

> This plaque is placed in memory of Sir Harold Ridley, FRS, 1906–2001, pioneer of intraocular lens surgery, graduate and benefactor of this college, after whose ancestor Bishop Nicholas Ridley, Master 1540–1553, martyred 1555, this path is traditionally named.

Intraocular lens surgery is better known as cataract surgery. Behind the pupil of the human eye is a lens which refracts and focuses light on to the retina, enabling us to see. Among the consequences of the ageing process is a tendency for cataracts to form on this lens. Most people aged over 60 will have some signs of cataracts without noticing them, but in some cases the cataracts will form a film, like ice on a windscreen on a frosty morning. This can lead to blindness. During the Battle of Britain in the summer of 1940 Harold Ridley was responsible for the care of aircrew whose eyes had been damaged in combat, usually by splinters from cockpit hoods. He observed that certain aircrew, notably Spitfire pilots, were much less liable to suffer allergic reactions than those with glass hoods. The Spitfire was exceptionally light and its hood was made from lightweight acrylic plastic.

After the war Ridley went into partnership with a company called Rayner to make artificial plastic lenses to replace the defective ones. Following an experimental temporary implant in 1949, on 8 February 1950 he performed the first permanent artificial lens implant at St Thomas' Hospital in London. The event is marked by a plaque at the hospital. The procedure remained controversial for many years, which may explain why Harold Ridley had to wait until he was 80 before being elected to the Royal Society, and 93 before receiving a knighthood. However, this is now the operation most frequently performed by the NHS, with almost half a million such procedures undertaken each year. Worldwide countless millions have their sight restored by an operation carried out by local anaesthetic in day surgery, taking between 20 and 30 minutes.

The Ridley Eye Foundation was established in 1967. The charity aimed to raise funds for cataract surgery and to promote better eye health in developing countries – including the treatment of River Blindness and blindness caused by snake venom from spitting cobras, in which he also did pioneering work. In 2000 the Royal Mail issued a series of commemorative stamps to mark medical breakthroughs. The 67p stamp commemorated 'artificial lens implant surgery pioneered by Sir Harold Ridley, 1949'.

Sir Harold Ridley had another claim to distinction. Before his death at the age of 94 in 2001, he had become the last living person to have met Florence Nightingale. She was a friend of his mother and he had met her at

the age of four; she died in 1910. But it is his groundbreaking work in the field of eye care that makes him a great benefactor to humankind as well as to his College. Of all the features of the College, the story of Harold Ridley and cataract operations makes one of the strongest impressions on visitors. Any group of adult visitors is likely to include people who have had the operation and will insist on testifying to its transformative influence on their lives.

RAY DOLBY AND THE MAGNOLIA GARDEN

Opposite the Ridley memorial lies a garden of magnolia trees, the first of many generous gifts to the College by the late Ray Dolby and his family. The garden was in memory of Meredith Dewey. The Dolby story prompts as strong a reaction among visitors as that of Harold Ridley.

Ray Dolby (1933–2013) came to Pembroke in 1957. His widow Dagmar has written in another chapter about his life at Cambridge (pp. 50–3). Upon completion of his PhD Dolby became a research fellow at Pembroke, a time on which he looked back with particular pleasure, before moving to London to found Dolby Laboratories with a staff of four.

Here they developed the Dolby Noise Reduction System with the aim of reducing, and eventually eliminating, the background hiss on recording tapes – something that those of mature years recall from the 1950s and 1960s. This work was far removed from his doctoral thesis, but it required a similar level of theoretical understanding and practical application. The first customer for the new system was Decca Records, who applied it to the recording of the pianist Vladimir Askenazy playing Mozart. The first patent application for the system was made in 1969.

The company moved to California in search of opportunities in the film industry. It settled in San Francisco and the first film to adopt the technique was *A Clockwork Orange* in 1971. Other films followed, and cinema-goers invariably now see a film credit to Dolby Sound. The system has been developed further to apply to DVDs, televisions, iPhones and computers. Dolby Laboratories in California now employs over 2,000 people.

The first reaction of visitors to the Dolby story is that they did not realise that Dolby was a person, having assumed it to be an acronym for a technical term. However, everyone knows what it does.

Two magnolia trees at the corner of New Court. Donated to the College by Ray Dolby in 1985, in memory of Meredith Dewey, they flower gloriously every year.

11 The Library at Pembroke

Mark Purcell

There has been a library at Pembroke for as long as the College has existed. The earliest version of the Statutes placed its books in the charge of a 'thesaurius' ('treasurer') or 'custos librorum' ('keeper of the books'), the earliest reference to a librarian in any Oxford or Cambridge College. The number of manuscripts would initially have been small. They were shared out annually among the Fellowship on or after the Feast of the Translation of St Thomas (7 July: the end of the academic year). The title of each book was written onto a parchment sheet on one side of a wooden diptych. The Keeper then ensured that the name of the Fellow to whom each was allocated was inscribed onto a wax tablet opposite, to be deleted when it was returned. Such a way of sharing out books (known as an 'electio') was typical of monastic and collegiate communities. At Pembroke, however, Fellows could also borrow books outside the 'electio' system, though they had to pay caution money.

The Library's Upper Reading Room, built by Waterhouse in 1878.

11 THE LIBRARY AT PEMBROKE 107

At first books would have been kept in chests alongside charters, the College seal and other valuables (the University's central fund is still known as 'the Chest'). However, by 1417 there was a library room at Pembroke. The College had paid out 11s 4d for calf skins (i.e. vellum) for binding, as well as purchasing chains to secure manuscripts to sloping desks or lecterns – a form of library furniture still to be seen at Lincoln Cathedral and, in later form, in the Elizabethan Old Library at Trinity Hall.

As more books were acquired space ran out, and in 1452 a 'new and magnificent library' was built above the Dining Hall. According to documents now lost but seen by Matthew Wren in the seventeenth century, the building cost £47 7s 4d and was funded by the Master, Laurence Booth, a future Archbishop of York. Its row of equidistant Gothic windows, clearly visible in the late seventeenth-century engraving of Old Court by David Loggan (see p. 16), hint at the configuration of the interior, which later served as the model for the library of Lady Margaret Beaufort's new foundation at St John's in 1516.

THE MANUSCRIPTS OF PEMBROKE

Pembroke still owns many of the manuscripts that formed the working library of its medieval Fellows. These were augmented in the sixteenth and seventeenth centuries by numerous printed books, as well as by more than 150 medieval manuscripts from the library of the dissolved abbey at Bury St Edmunds. Some of the later acquisitions, such as the twelfth-century *Bury Gospels* (Pembroke MS 120), are very remarkable indeed. The group as a whole is the largest that has survived from one of the greatest Benedictine houses in Europe.

Following all these additions, the library room of 1452 was completely refitted by Matthew Wren in 1617, following his complaint that the books had been damaged by the sloping form of the library desks and the weight of the chains. A new set of library regulations followed in 1622, while Wren's splendidly illuminated Benefactors' Book (now digitised and available on the Cambridge Digital Library) is a key document, recording information about the provenance of items in the library for which the original records have now been lost. The arrangement and contents of the library in this period could in fact be reconstructed in detail. Not only do we have many of the books but also a detailed catalogue, compiled in 1663, presumably part of

The Nuremberg Chronicle *showing illustrations of Popes and Roman emperors. It has been extensively annotated by a previous owner.*

A detail from the Bury Gospels; *a decorated capital 'B' from the letter of St Jerome to Pope Damasus.*

A page from Matthew Wren's Benefactors' Book. The leaves of the golden tree are inscribed with the names of donors to the College.

A page from the Bury Gospels showing three scenes from the life of Christ.

setting the College in order after the Restoration. Some months earlier the College Meeting had agreed that duplicate books could be sold, and reminded Fellows to sign out books as per statute or face a fine of 5s. By then the book chains had gone: in comparison with Oxford, where the Old Library at Magdalen was still chained in 1799, Cambridge unchained early.

With the completion of the new Chapel which Matthew Wren commissioned from his nephew Christopher, the College's ancient chapel, dedicated to the Holy Trinity and located since the fourteenth century just to the left of the main gate, was left empty. In 1673 the College set aside four substantial donations for the library, totalling £480. Finally, in August 1688, the Fellowship made a decision and ordered 'that the Old Chapel be converted to a Library'. The task of planning the move, carried out by three of the Fellows, began in February 1693. It was completed in 1697, with the books lodged on magnificent carved book cases (two of which still survive), closely related to similar cases once in the Old University Library and in other Cambridge Colleges. A carpenter was paid £36 on the orders of the Master, the Cornishman Nathaniel Coga, in 1690.

The splendid ceiling, by the London plasterer Henry Doogood, dates from the same year, rich in iconography alluding to books, learning and hunting (the quest for knowledge?) and with the arms of William and Mary and of the Foundress on the east wall. Again the arrangement, contents and functioning of the library in the 180 years it occupied what is now known as 'the Old Library' could largely be reconstructed – we have the books, multiple catalogues and a borrowing register (a page for each Fellow: this was still very much a library for the Fellows). There is also a very detailed set of library accounts, signed off annually by the Master at the Audit Meeting and running from 1695 to 1933. The accounts reveal a wealth of detail about the health of the library fund (known as 'the Library Bag'), revenues from endowments and the activities of the Library Keeper and other Fellows (more happening in the early eighteenth century than the early nineteenth). The accounts also record the purchasing, carriage and binding of books, the receipt of gifts and updating of the Benefactors' Book, the costs of compiling catalogues and engraving and printing bookplates with the College arms, the undertaking of repairs to panelling, windows and library globes, and even payments for dusting.

A page from the Bury Gospels *featuring the beginning of the Gospel of St Matthew. The beautifully decorated initial is an 'L'.*

The Library Clocktower, with Red Buildings, by Alfred Waterhouse to the right. The Library drew inspiration from a Flemish town hall; Red Buildings from a French château.

THE NEW LIBRARY BUILDING

The present Library building was part of the great rebuilding of Pembroke by the Manchester architect Alfred Waterhouse. Waterhouse's assertive brand of Gothic Revival was popular in mid-Victorian Cambridge; he did work at Caius and Trinity Hall, as well as designing the Natural History Museum in London (1873–80) and Manchester Town Hall (1877). At Pembroke other issues were in play as well as architectural fashion, including the election of an ambitious young Master, John Power, in 1870. By then a College building fund had been accumulating for over 80 years and stood at some £70,000; there was also a generous bequest of £500 for the library from the Reverend Henry Tasker, Vicar of Soham, in 1873. With university reform in the air, some may have feared for all this money if it remained unspent, while the ten years of Power's Mastership saw undergraduate numbers dramatically increase.

Waterhouse's demolition of the fourteenth-century Hall and the old Master's lodgings, and plans to mete out a similar treatment to the Wren Chapel and the Old Library, proved deeply controversial, ultimately precipitating his dismissal by the College in 1879. However, his new Library, with lecture rooms underneath, was at least on a new site and did not entail the destruction of anything else. Stylistically it is a mix of Gothic Revival and French or Flemish Renaissance, finely finished – now a familiar part of the Pembroke landscape, but once startling. Waterhouse's final account was for £13,130 6s 11d. The great majority of this was for work done between 1876 and 1879 by the Cambridge building contractors Rattee and Kett, though £476 15s went on glazing and more than £200 was spent on the clock.

The new Library opened in 1879, when the books were moved across from its predecessor, at a cost of £10 8s 4½d. From here on Library accounts suggest an altogether different approach from earlier times, reflective of the College that Pembroke was becoming in the latter part of the nineteenth century. A full-time Library Assistant (later titled Assistant Librarian) was employed. Expenditure on books increased, sometimes with London dealers such as Maggs and Quaritch, but usually from the Cambridge bookseller Deighton Bell, suggesting mostly recent publications. There was the implied expectation that the College's new and much larger Library, closely associated with lecture rooms, would be used by Pembroke's

An autumnal rainbow over the illuminated Library.

expanding population of undergraduates, who paid an admission fee from 1895. No longer was it the preserve of a small group of Fellows.

Yet despite the enormous expansion of the College over the following century, Waterhouse's building survived largely unaltered until the 1990s. Work then undertaken by the Cambridge architect Tristan Rhys-Roberts provided better access to the upper floor, additional shelving and student work places, meeting rooms, a law library and underground storage for the College's archives and rare books. It also created a spectacular stained-glass window, honouring the long-standing College commitment that the neighbouring garden of the Master of Peterhouse would not be overlooked. In tandem, with Victoriana back in fashion, Waterhouse's building and furnishings received some much needed care and attention.

LOOKING INTO THE FUTURE

It is intriguing to speculate what might happen next. For the historic collections, much has been achieved in recent years. The College's wonderful medieval manuscripts, kept at the University Library since 1968, have recently been described in magisterial detail in a new catalogue by Professor Rod Thomson, published in 2021. An obvious next step might be to digitise them, but this is expensive – and would certainly require conservation support to protect the many original medieval bindings. The College Archive is now visible on Archives Search, the cross-Cambridge online archive catalogue (2020), though most of the archive is not yet catalogued online. The rare books, too, are being slowly catalogued online. However, their visibility in the College remains low and much remains to be done to make them genuinely accessible for research (among countless other treasures, the early books include most of the library of Lancelot Andrewes, as well as important material acquired more recently).

In addition, a response is needed to what most would now consider the prime purpose of a college library: that of providing study space and the first port of call for printed books for many undergraduates, along with advice and support on study and research skills. There is now a widespread assumption that students want a wider range of library spaces (multipurpose 'hub' spaces, informal and group study spaces are appearing all over the University, for example), and there is a growing reliance, especially since the Covid-19 pandemic, on electronic resources – accessible from anywhere in the world and supplied in Cambridge by the University Library. Already much has changed since the last round of changes in the 1990s. It will be interesting to see how the College's Library buildings, and the way in which they are used, will evolve in the next generation.

A detail of the 'weesle headed armadillo', based on an illustration in Nehemiah Grew's 1681 work Musaeum Regalis Societatis.

Opposite *Within the Upper Reading Room; Waterhouse's stained glass and a bust of William Pitt.*

12 The Cloisters

James Gardom and Elizabeth Ennion-Smith

Old Court from the Cloisters. The brass plaques on the columns commemorate those who lost their lives in the Second World War.

The Cloisters, which today form part of the west side of Old Court, was completed by Christmas 1666. When first built, it actually comprised the west side of Chapel Court. What we know today as Old Court was then two courts, divided by a range of buildings knocked down in 1874 to make today's larger Old Court. The structure originally consisted of a cloister on the ground floor and two floors of rooms above. The arms of Robert Hitcham appear on the panel on the court side, as much of the cost was covered by his benefaction of 1636.

Consecrated separately but on the same day as the main Chapel (21 September 1665), and a little before it was fully completed, the Cloisters provided a link between Chapel Court and Old Court and a doorway onto Trumpington Street. Both the antechapel, the Cell under the east end of the Chapel and the Cloisters were also designated places of burial: Fellows in the antechapel, Matthew Wren in the Cell and students in the Cloisters. This was a necessary requirement in the late seventeenth century when bouts of plague were common and sending a body back to distant parts of the country for burial at home was impossible.

The Cloisters changed firstly with the demolition in 1874 of the old Master's Lodge and the south range of Old Court, suddenly becoming part of a much larger court. Another change occurred in 1881, with the extension of the Chapel by George Gilbert Scott Jr. As well as extending the Chapel, the Cloisters were reduced in width by the addition of a row of small rooms on the west (street) side and new staircases to provide access to the rooms above.

COMMEMORATION IN THE CLOISTERS

Change in the Cloisters continued in the twentieth century, following the addition in 1924 of the First World War Memorial and then in 1948 with memorial plaques for those killed in the Second World War. Several designs were considered for the First World War Memorial,

Details from the War Memorial for the students and staff of Pembroke who died in the First World War. Student names are listed by year of matriculation.

The First World War Memorial, installed in the Cloisters in 1924.

including a standalone memorial in the centre of Old Court more akin to the Cambridge City memorial. However, the Cloisters seemed the most appropriate site, with its proximity to the Chapel and prominent location in College. Designed by Thomas Henry Lyon (then Director of Design at the Cambridge School of Architecture) and carved in Portland stone, the memorial is striking for its egalitarianism – those recorded are listed not by rank but by year of 'belonging to the College',[1] with members of staff, then known as College servants, listed at the end. It was dedicated on 3 December 1924 by the Bishop of Wakefield.

Facing the First World War Memorial is a series of five bronze plaques upon which the names of the fallen of the Second World War are inscribed. Designed by Murray Easton, the series of plaques forming the Memorial was paid for by subscription, as part of the War Memorial and Sexcentenary Appeal. It was dedicated at a service held in the Chapel on 10 July 1948. The layout echoes that of the First World War Memorial, with regiments listed rather than ranks, and names arranged by matriculation year. College staff are again incorporated on the memorial.

There is an interesting diversity of names and regiments, particularly in the First World War Memorial. The eye is caught by K.I. Singh of the Indian Medical Service, E.V. Hemmant of the East Africa Volunteer Force, H. Southern of the Indian Army Reserve of Officers, C.G. Napier of the 35th Sikhs Indian Army, A.H. Ramsay of the French Army and C.J. Wright Ingle of the Royal Fusiliers Leinster Regiment.

The first Pembroke casualty of the First World War seems to have been Corporal Henry Good Fielding Johnson from the Royal Engineers.

---

1 Research done in 2018 by Michael Kuczynski noted the initial uncertainty surrounding what constituted membership of Pembroke College. A record in the College Meeting minute of 21 October 1919 notes that it was agreed to include 'all accepted candidates for entrance at the College although they might not have actually come into residence'.

Sunlight within the Cloisters. The First World War Memorial is to the left, the series of plaques forming the Second World War memorial is to the right.

He completed a year of study at Pembroke. It is a little unclear how he managed to become a signals officer close to the frontline by 23 August 1914, only three weeks after the beginning of the war. One speculation is that he may have gained rapid deployment and promotion by supplying his own motorcycle.

In *Martlet* (Spring 2014), Ian Westerman's account of the Corporal's last days is poignant, and helps to evoke something of the innumerable individual stories that lie behind the list of names.

5th Division Signal Company War Diary records that by 12th August the war establishment of 12 motorcyclists, with their machines, had mobilised and were undergoing musketry training in Carlow. The Company entrained for Dublin on 15th and arrived in Le Havre at about 5pm on the 17th. There they were accommodated in 'M' shed of the Magasin General and rested until being required to parade at the railway station on the 19th. From Le Havre they went by train to Landrecies and were billeted in a barracks there. Over the next 4 days they were constantly on the move and having to establish communications from the Divisional HQ both to their brigades and to GHQ II Corps, the motorcycle dispatch riders being used for the latter task. The BEF had its first contact with the enemy on the 22nd, although this was mainly light skirmishing, the conflict proper not beginning until the following day. On the morning of the 23rd the 5th Division HQ was in Dour and the Signal Company had established itself at the railway station, wherever possible making using of the permanent telegraph system that was in place as they also had operators at the stations at Hamin and Boussu. The remainder of communications were sent by dispatch rider. The following day the Company sent two men to Patourages railway station to try to establish communications there for the 15th Brigade, which they did. The War Diary records that they remained there despite the village being under heavy fire until forced to withdraw when the station itself began to take hits. A few lines later the War Diary reads: 'One motorcyclist (Cpl Fielding-Johnson) went out from DOUR with a dispatch, and has not since been heard of by me'. His body was never found.

Over the centenary years the College put Royal British Legion crosses in the Cloisters as close as possible to the centenaries of the individual deaths.

The memorial to Pembroke students who were citizens of the Central Powers and died in the First World War: 'Here, too, glory has its rewards'.

The Cloisters from Old Court built in the seventeenth century, contemporaneously with the Chapel.

The Fellows also resolved to put in a memorial to members of the College who died in the Armed Forces of the Central Powers. Because of the disruption of the records caused by the Second World War, it was not possible to produce a comprehensive list of names, so the text of the memorial reads:

> In Memory of Members of this College
> Citizens of the Central Powers
> Who fought and died for their countries in the War 1914–1918.
> SUNT HIC ETIAM SUA PRAEMIA LAUDI

The Latin epitaph was suggested by Michael Kuczynski. It comes from Virgil's *Aeneid*, at a point where Aeneas is looking at murals of Priam and the Trojan War in Carthage. A recent translation, including the next phrase, reads 'Here too, glory has its rewards; the world weeps, and mortal matters move the heart'.[2]

2 Bartsch, Shadi (trans.). *The Aeneid*. New ed. 2020.

Part IV
Art and Life

13 The Art of Pembroke

Polly Blakesley

Portrait of Sir John Sulston, Nobel Prize Winner in Physiology and Medicine, by Tom Phillips RA, 2004. © Tom Phillips. All Rights Reserved, DACS 2024

In the late twentieth century Pembroke's art collection, while blessed with paintings of and by eminent figures, would not have distinguished itself from those of many Oxbridge Colleges. Thankfully a growing appetite to refresh and extend the collection, together with the benefaction of members and alumni, has led to spectacular acquisitions in recent years.

RECENT PORTRAIT COMMISSIONS

A perfect opportunity to commission a new portrait arose in 2002, when Honorary Fellow Sir John Sulston was awarded a joint Nobel Prize in Physiology and Medicine. While Pembroke has taken pride in two previous Nobel laureates (former graduate student Rodney Robert Porter, for Chemistry in 1972, and Visiting Scholar William Fowler, for Physics in 1983), Sulston was the first former undergraduate to receive the award. With generous support from Fellow Commoner Randall Dillard, the College commissioned Tom Phillips RA to paint his portrait.

Portrait of Kamau Brathwaite, Caribbean writer and poet, by Errol Lloyd, 2019.

Phillips chose to position Sulston against a web of diagrams taken from the geneticist's research notes on the nematode worm. However, he feared he had misjudged the relation between the figure and background by placing Sulston too low down in the painting. An inventive solution presented itself when, while meeting for a sitting at Phillips's home on 8 June 2004, the two men wandered into the garden to watch the Transit of Venus, the first to take place since 1882. As Phillips later recounted, their shared experience of this rare astronomical event inspired him to introduce the black dot against a circular segment at the top right of the picture. This act both resolved the compositional imbalance and created a portrait that honours the generative moments of friendship as much as it does the heights of professional success.

Sulston's portrait heralded other notable arrivals on Pembroke's walls. Bryan Organ devised a striking bipartite arrangement in his portrait of former Master, Sir Richard Dearlove, replete with Delphic references to Sir Richard's previous career as head of MI6. The acquisition of Peter Edwards's portrait of Ted Hughes provided the perfect partner to hang opposite that of Sulston, bookending the diners at High Table with lodestars in the sciences and the arts.

These were soon joined by Errol Lloyd's portrait of Kamau Brathwaite, the Barbadian poet and powerhouse of Caribbean literature who had been elected an Honorary Fellow in 2016. Jamaican-born Lloyd had sketched Brathwaite, a founder of the Caribbean Artists Movement, some 30 years previously. In 2019 he travelled to Barbados to carry out preliminary studies for the Pembroke commission. Painted in profile with a shimmering base palette of ochres and yellows, Brathwaite's image illuminates those around it with its vibrant energy and quietly reflective gaze.

In another watershed moment, Isabella Watling showcased the professional stature of Honorary Fellow and world-renowned clarinettist Emma Johnson by portraying her in concert dress with clarinet at the ready. Women artists were already represented (just) in the collection, notably by Annalivia Limb's posthumous bronze head of Ted Hughes and Daphne Todd's portrait of Richard Adrian, the Master who oversaw the decision in 1982 to admit women to study at Pembroke. (The first women undergraduates arrived in 1984.) But Johnson's picture marked the first time the College had commissioned a painted portrait of a woman in the course of some 650 years.

Jo Cox MP, murdered in 2016, portrait by Clara Drummond, 2022.

PORTRAITS OF WOMEN AT PEMBROKE

Johnson's portrait provided that of the Foundress with welcome female company, but the dearth of paintings of women in Pembroke remained acute. While far from redressing the balance, two signal acquisitions shed a spotlight on other remarkable alumnae. In the first case, Clara Drummond was commissioned to paint a posthumous portrait of the murdered MP Jo Cox. Pembroke is indebted to Jo's family and friends, who supported this initiative despite the fact that Jo, from a northern working-class background and the first of her family to go to university, had found life at Pembroke in the early 1990s far from easy.

Jo, who died in 2016, stood for the values of equality, tolerance and civilised debate that many felt had been imperilled by the torrid nature of public discourse at the time. Drawing inspiration from the work of the Renaissance artist Sandro Botticelli and with a nod to the flowers of Jo's wedding bouquet, Drummond's luminescent portrait emphatically avoids any reference to that polarised political landscape. Instead it embodies the clarity of vision and purpose that guided Jo's life.

If Cox's portrait is consciously apolitical, that of Honorary Fellow Vicky Bowman CMG, who served as British Ambassador to Myanmar before becoming Director of the Myanmar Centre for Responsible Business, engages directly with socio-political concerns. Bowman's husband, the artist and former political prisoner Htein Lin, portrays her in an array of patterns summoned in proud, visceral impasto. At the top of the canvas, a slogan in thick white brushstrokes alludes to traditional gendered attitudes in Myanmar that Bowman found to be shifting among her in-laws. One of the most technically adventurous of Pembroke's paintings, it animates its surroundings with its effusion of colour and suggestive commentary.

After serving as British Ambassador to Myanmar, Vicky Bowman remained in Myanmar to advocate for responsible business. She was imprisoned by the military regime in 2022, as was her husband, the artist Htein Lin, then released a few months later. This portrait of Vicky was painted by her husband.

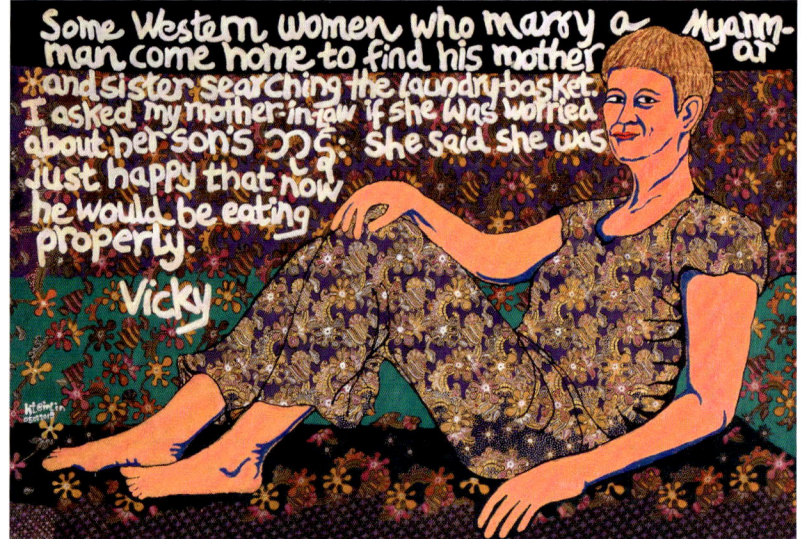

ARTWORKS ON THE MILL LANE SITE

The portraits discussed above usually hang in the Dining Hall, but Pembroke's expansion on the Mill Lane site has created exciting prospects for artists. Providing welcome contrast to the figurative images that dominate the College's older collections, Indigenous Australian artist George Tjungurrayi's richly gestural abstract painting commands attention in one of the elegant new interiors of the Mill Lane development. It is a generous gift from the Myer and Baillieu family in Australia, marking four generations of Pembroke affiliation.

In other cases artworks were not just acquired for Pembroke's new buildings but evolved with them symbiotically, forming part of the very fabric of the place. Alison Turnbull, appointed lead artist of the Mill Lane project and working in situ while construction was underway, has produced a tour de force of site-specific work in her installation in Chiu Court. Making ingenious use of overlooked drawings in the College archives, Turnbull introduced a porcelain mosaic inspired by the spiral patterns in designs that the nineteenth-century architect Alfred Waterhouse produced for the staircase in Pembroke Library. Around the mosaic, skilful York Stone paving creates a Voronoi pattern devised by the artist in consultation with some of Pembroke's scientists.

Ignoring the furore of construction work all around her, Turnbull also painted two abstract geometric frescoes directly onto the plasterwork at either end of the foyer to the Auditorium. These are complemented on the mezzanine floor above by 'light paintings' – works made in glass by Valencian Ardyn Halter, whose generosity has already enriched the College with a set of his intensely hued abstract landscapes.

Alison Turnbull's work of art in the centre of Chiu Court includes two mosaic basins that trickle water across the whole piece.

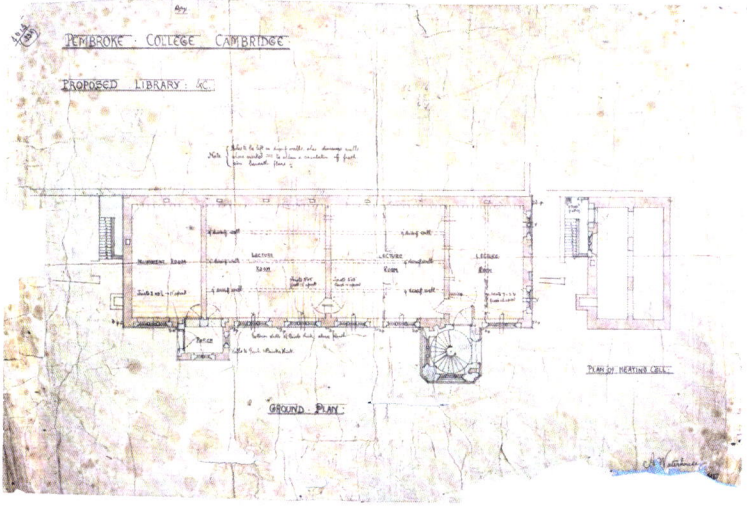

Above *An artwork by Alison Turnbull in Chiu Court. The design of the central mosaic is drawn from Waterhouse's original drawings for the spiral staircase in the Library tower (**right**).*

Opposite *The stained-glass window designed by the artist Ardyn Halter, in the balcony above the foyer beside the Auditorium. The window is based on the colours of the Pembroke College crest.*

Rarely has the case for interdisciplinary and multimedial artistry been more forcefully made than in Mill Lane's embedded artworks.

THE NEW EXHIBITION SPACE

The opening of Phase 1 of the Mill Lane site in 2023 included the launch of its glorious new exhibition space. For the inaugural exhibition, *Engaging Pembroke*, three Cambridge-based artists, Xinyi Bi, Rebecca Ilett and Idit Nathan, were invited to respond to the brief of 'bringing Pembroke College's site, spaces, history and communities into dialogue with the work of contemporary artists'. Their imaginative responses generate new insights into the work of the College and its physical presence, inviting audiences to consider both familiar and revelatory aspects of Pembroke life.

Xinyi Bi's five pictures – devised through paint, print and collage – capture the College's distinctive spirit from various vantage points. In so doing, they weave a visual narrative that resonates both with viewers familiar with Pembroke's spaces and those encountering them for the first time. Depicting the Auditorium, Chapel, Library, Old Court and Garden, they explore Pembroke's navigation of old and new, together with its commitment to a judicious balance between tradition and change.

Jeweller and sculptor Rebecca Ilett's miniature silver models representing the Chapel and Library reflect her excitement in some of the maps and architects' drawings in Pembroke's archives. Altering the scale of the buildings allows the viewer to rethink the relationship between human and architectural scale, and to discover or reconsider aspects of a built environment that they may have thought they already knew well. Creating an imaginative response rather than replicas, Ilett makes play with perception and reality, inscribing exquisite detail on the shadow of the miniature Chapel rather than on its walls.

Finally Idit Nathan, a conceptual artist, was inspired by a slow and contemplative walk around Pembroke to produce a series of prints, each accompanied by a Braille sign, entitled *Feeling the Way*. Exploring the shifting dialogue between history, meaning and materiality, Idit reimagines the walk via a sequence of five word pairs, one of which appears on each print. The word pairs are deliberately obscured within a web of lines on the prints, but are provided in Braille on the signs beneath. They thus require viewers to deploy visual detective skills and/or a sense of touch to enable the words to surface and make sense. Particularly compelling is that visually impaired viewers with knowledge of Braille can access the words more easily than those with unimpaired sight, raising questions

Rebecca Ilett's beautiful miniature silver sculpture of Pembroke's Chapel, specially created for the opening exhibition for the Mill Lane site.

Henry Moore's sculpture, Figure in a Shelter, *on loan to the College from the Henry Moore Foundation. Its curvaceous form contrasts perfectly with the rectangular facade of Foundress Court behind.*

about accessibility and inclusivity that resonate with Pembroke's driving priorities.

Alongside the work of these artists, the exhibition *Engaging Pembroke* included objects from Pembroke's historic collections: former Dean Meredith Dewey's mineral collection, whose gemstone palette resonates in several works generated for Mill Lane; and the wooden model of Christopher Wren's Chapel. The curiosity these inspire in artists and visitors alike reminds us of the constant stimulus afforded by Pembroke's breathtaking settings and artefacts, and the value of revisiting traditions even as we seek to renew.

OUTDOOR SCULPTURE

Over the past nine years, the sculpture collection of the College has been gradually expanded, enhancing the interaction of buildings and gardens around Pembroke. Three of these works have been generously lent to the College as long-term loans: *Figure in a Shelter*, a late sculpture by Henry Moore, on loan from the Henry Moore Foundation and curvaceously set against the rectangular facade of Foundress Court; Nigel Hall's *Natural Pearl*, whose swooping circles in corten steel offset the seventeenth-century buildings on either side of Ivy Court; and *Close* by Antony Gormley – an unmistakable Gormley figure that leans into the facade of Milstein House as if seeking shelter within. All three are wonderful additions to Pembroke's buildings and gardens.

Inspired by the arrival of the Henry Moore, alumnus Harry Howard has also handsomely gifted three further works. These include *Crescent Figure* by John Farnham (who worked with Moore), which we initially placed outside the Library on a temporary basis, with the installation supervised by Farnham himself. However, the unanimous view of everyone in the College was that *Crescent Figure* suited that location so perfectly that it had to remain there for posterity. Harry Howard then donated *Crown of Thorns*, a sculpture in aluminium by Austin Wright which is now attached to the wall of Foundress Court facing Tennis Court Road, adjacent to the Butler Gates; and William Pye's *Triple Loop*, a small cascade of stainless steel that now sits in the corner of Red Buildings Lawn.

All of these sculptures help to bring art into the spaces and gardens of the College. They provide a perfect accompaniment to the courtyards, lawns and foliage which are part of the glory of Pembroke. We are infinitely the richer for them.

Triple Loop (1978), a stainless-steel sculpture by William Pye, cascades amidst the foliage beside Red Buildings Lawn.

Antony Gormley's sculpture in cast iron, Close (2024), on loan to Pembroke from the artist. At the College it will lean into the front wall of Milstein House.

Crescent Figure *by John Farnham, outside the Library at Pembroke.*

Overleaf *Ivy Court looking towards the Orchard. In the foreground to the right is Nigel Hall's* Natural Pearl *sculpture in corten steel.*

13 THE ART OF PEMBROKE

14 Room N8B

Mark Wormald

Pembroke has every kind of room – as grand, intimate, bright, old, new and quirky as the ideas and feelings they have held. But only one has entered literary history, and even literary myth. Welcome to N8B, a large, if rather dark, north-facing room whose two tall windows look out towards Pembroke Street over the Fellows' car park.

Originally part of a grand first-floor suite in Alfred Waterhouse's Master's Lodge, reached from a landing off the imposing stairs that rise from the lobby outside the College bar, Room N8B itself has had a curious history. By 1951, the rest of the suite was a Fellow's set: economic historian David Joslin moved in on his election that year. So the door connecting N8's inner hallway and what became a student study bedroom was doubled and locked. For five years from 1992, when I had N8B as my own study, I barely noticed it. Nor, I confess, did I then question the room's real architectural oddity, which must have dated from that decision to divide the suite: my front door. Surely not part of Waterhouse's design, its peculiar position probably reflected bursarial thrift, avoiding the expense of rerouting the original pipework, itself long gone by my day. At any rate, to reach N8B from the landing I climbed three steps up to the threshold, opened the door inwards, then descended three steps into the room: an unforgettable commute.

After I moved out, our Development team moved in. N8's unity was restored, the connecting door reopened. Since 2012 several colleagues have worked there in brightly lit efficiency. That year a carpenter removed the three steps down into my former den, to accommodate a filing cabinet of alumni records and latterly a bookcase. That front door, left high and dry mid-wall behind it, has not opened in a decade.

But once it did, momentously. In 1952–3 Joslin's neighbour was a second-year undergraduate reading English: 'Hughes, E.J.', according to the leather-bound Schedule of Rooms. The world knows him as the poet Ted

Opposite *A stained-glass window in honour of Ted Hughes by Hans von Stockhausen in the Library's Yamada Room. Hughes's desk and chair are featured in the foreground.*

Hughes. An encounter he had one April night in N8B made him change course, affected his life as well as his degree, and inspired a poem that has become an emblem of the strange and vivid life of poetry itself. Hughes spoke and wrote of it again and again, in private conversations, letters, poetry readings, on television and in print. Against sceptics, he always insisted on its 'total reality'. He wrote his last and definitive account, 'The Burnt Fox', in 1993, when I was in N8B.

It began with something mundane enough: an essay crisis. Hughes needed to write one last weekly essay before his Part I examinations and he liked its subject, Samuel Johnson, so got started on it early. But three or four agonising days and nights followed; he just could not get beyond the first few lines. Forty years on, seven after returning to Pembroke as Poet Laureate to receive an Honorary Doctorate, he recalled the scene with startling clarity.

Portrait of Ted Hughes, Poet Laureate, by Peter Edwards, 1993.

> My desk lamp light fell on the paper. Close to my left was my high curtained window. In front of me, beyond my table, was my bed, the head at the far end. To my right, across the room, were the three wooden steps that climbed to my door, on which hung my gown. At last I had to give up and go to bed.
>
> It was 2 a.m.

Hughes dreamed. He was back at that desk, bent over the lamplit paper, when 'Suddenly my attention was drawn to the door'. It opened slowly; a head came round its edge, at 'about the height of a man's head, but clearly the head of a fox'. Down those three stairs and across the room, towards him, 'came a figure that was at the same time a skinny man and a fox walking erect on its hind legs'. As this 'creature' – sometimes, in the telling of it, 'he', but not yet in this last version – entered the brighter light of the desk lamp, Hughes 'saw that its body had just now stepped out of a furnace'. The whole body was charred, 'split and bleeding'; 'its eyes', levelling with Hughes at his desk, 'dazzled with the intensity of pain'.

> Then it spread its hand – a human hand, as I now saw, but burned and bleeding like the rest of him [– him! –] flat palm down on the blank space of my page.

Then the creature spoke: 'Stop this – you are destroying us.' As that hand lifted away, it left a 'blood-print, like a palmist's specimen, with all the lines and creases, in wet, glistening blood on the page'.

Hughes took dreams seriously. He connected 'the fox's command', as he described it to his closest critic Keith Sagar in 1979, 'to my own ideas about Eng. Lit.' as Cambridge in the fifties had marked them, and to himself.

> Leavis-style dismantling of texts … seemed to me not only a foolish game, but deeply destructive of myself.

So by 'destroying us', the creature meant: you and me both.

Hughes listened, then acted. He switched to Archaeology and Anthropology in his final year; even before then, the release was immediate. Staying in College during the long vacation, he moved into an attic set of rooms, E1, 'the loveliest room in the world', directly above the Old Library. He spent the small hours of the night painting 'enormous red and green leopards on the wall', as he wrote to his brother Gerald that summer. No other trace of these creatures remains: Tony Camps, Pembroke's Tutor, insisted that they be whitewashed over, at his expense. Which may be why, in that 1979 letter to Sagar, Hughes covered his own tracks as he did, laying a false trail. The room where he dreamed of the burned fox was, he wrote, 'on K staircase, 1st floor'. Those, as I discovered from that Schedule, were Mr Camps's rooms.

In December 1955, working in London, Hughes returned through a snowy night to his

Room N8, Ted Hughes's room, as it now is, with the door finally opened.

lodgings and to another 'blank page where my fingers move'. He wrote, 'in a few minutes', he later claimed, his poem 'The Thought-Fox'. Find it, read it, listen online to Hughes reading it. He honours that strange compound creature by restoring it to delicate life: from 'A fox's nose' via 'Two eyes [that] serve a movement, that now / And again now, and now, and now / Sets neat prints into the snow,' to the moment when with 'a sudden sharp hot stink of fox / It enters the dark hole of the head' and 'The page is printed'.

In 1986 Hughes told an audience in New York that this was the first poem he 'kept', and that it also 'commemorates my departure from studies of academic English'. Other foxes marked the poem: one he met at dawn as a teenager in South Yorkshire. A second that 'intruded' from a Swedish film he had just seen in which a fox comes through a snowy wood towards the camera, its eyes ablaze. But read it again: 'a lame / Shadow lags'. 'Looking backwards,' Hughes said, he was 'more and more sure of the third fox behind it.' That Pembroke fox, the burnt fox.

It lives still. When in 2000 Pembroke commissioned Hans Gottfried von Stockhausen's stained-glass windows in Hughes's honour for the College Library's Yamada Room, a panel devoted to 'The Thought-Fox' became essential – complete with its own shocking bloodprint of a human hand.

Above *Room on the first floor of K staircase, originally thought to have been Hughes's room.*

Opposite *Looking south into seventeenth-century Ivy Court from the first floor of K Staircase. Nigel Hall's sculpture* Natural Pearl *can be glimpsed through the window*

15 The Pembroke Smoking Concert

Eric Idle

In former days there was a performance space called the Old Reader underneath the College Library – and in it the Pembroke Players produced plays and 'Smokers', which were comedy nights. The Pembroke Players still do so, though the Old Reader has long since ceased to exist as a venue and of course no one now smokes during the show.

Here Eric Idle here writes about the 'Smokers' of old.

Pembroke College changed my life and I am very grateful for it. Because of Pembroke, and in particular the Pembroke Smoking Concert, I accidentally stumbled across what I would spend the rest of my life doing: writing and performing comedy. In October 1962 I was a shy boy escaping from being locked up for 12 years in a grim charity boarding school in Wolverhampton.

'Wolverhampton: not quite the end of the world, but you can see it from there…'

Little did I know at the time, but I was very fortunate to be going to the premiere Cambridge Comedy College; Pembroke had a long comedy tradition and its annual 'Smoker' was always sold out for three nights. It had been only five years since the great Peter Cook had reduced everyone to giggling heaps. A Pembroke alumnus, people were still doing Peter Cook voices.

'Sadly I was an only twin.'

'I'd like to invent something really important: like fire.'

'I could have been a Judge, but I didn't have the Latin. So I became a Miner instead. It's much easier to become a Miner than a Judge. They only ask you one question: What is your name? And I got fifty per cent on that.'

Later in life I was lucky enough to get to know the great Peter Cook. Once, on location in Mexico, we were bobbing up and down in the pool, when Peter asked:

'We all know the speed of light, Eric, but tell me what is the speed of darkness?'

Above *Eric Idle.*

Above right *Peter Cook.*

It seems no coincidence that England, a land rich in absurdities, should be so rich in comedians. Yet it's odd that so many were at Pembroke...

Writing about comedy is difficult, but it is not half so difficult as writing comedy. If I'm wrong when I'm writing *about* comedy then nobody cares, but if I'm wrong when I'm writing comedy then – horror of horrors – nobody laughs. It is this potential for disaster that gives comedy its edge. It is like tightrope walking. You really have to do it to know it, and indeed that is also the only way to learn how to do it. It is certainly a very odd activity. To stand on a stage before hundreds of other people and make them laugh is a very strange thing to do. Clearly when someone goes to such lengths to attract the admiration of strangers we can observe that they must feel desperately unloved, but this does not explain why we, the audience, should tolerate and actively encourage them in their weird behaviour. Nor why comedy should prove to be so popular or so universal. But it is a shared experience. Without an audience it is nothing. Far more so than tragedy, comedy is intimately connected with the audience's response. We weep alone, but we all laugh together. It is this shared communality that makes it so powerful and so popular. It is constantly reminding us of our own absurdity in this vast universe. It is frequently to do with scale, cutting us down to size, laughing at our human weaknesses. For a few moments

15 THE PEMBROKE SMOKING CONCERT

it removes us from the prison of our own personalities, the trap of our own self-created selves, and unites us in a warm shared response by making us laugh at the trivia in which we continually enmesh ourselves. It is an uplifting experience. We are taken out of ourselves, and made to laugh at ourselves. This is both slightly painful (laughing does hurt) and healthy (because it is done communally). It is instant group therapy.

It achieves this effect by demonstration rather than persuasion. We do not decide to laugh, we suddenly find ourselves laughing. In the dark amidst hundreds of strangers we are united in a tribal explosion of noise, which begins in a shout of recognition and ends in the sound of a gurgling drain or a goose being strangled. For a few seconds we are all barking sane together.

To be on the other side of a laugh, causing it, triggering it and feeling the great wave of approval come back at you, is one of the most powerful and addictive sensations there is: a great welcoming sound that wraps around the performer, enmeshing them in support. They can learn to play with it, to toy with the audience's expectations, to tickle the laugh, to surf along it, hold it back and then finally release it, but they can only learn this by doing it. To be sure, such ability is partly instinctive – some people *are* just funny – but it can also be learned, or at least honed and improved by experience. This is why a structure like the Cambridge Footlights is so useful. It is both a training ground, and a safety net, which prevents hundreds of people who are drawn to it but are otherwise unsuitable from pursuing comedy too far.

Of course, having escaped 12 years in a boarding school, my first concern arriving at

Tim Brooke-Taylor.

Cambridge was to ditch my involuntary state of chastity. In pursuit of this dream, in my first term I joined the Pembroke Players and appeared in a production of Strindberg's *The Father* in the Old Reader. Sadly, my social life did not significantly change immediately. No young aspiring actresses threw themselves across my path. However, things began to look up at the Pembroke Players Christmas party for which I wrote and performed a cabaret with two other guys in my staircase, a send-up of their recent production of Brecht's *The Caucasian Chalk Circle*. This was greeted so well by aspiring actors and actresses alike that I was told I should try out for the Pembroke Smoker. I had never heard of it. Word had not yet reached Wolverhampton that comedy was the key to successful mating, but I was beginning to enjoy being laughed at. It turned out that a

Smoking Concert is a College revue, in this case held annually in the Old Reader, a large room underneath the Library and so, a week later, I auditioned for Tim Brooke-Taylor and Bill Oddie in Tim's digs on Trumpington Street. I went in with two guys from the Pembroke Players and they threw the other two out and kept me. But, unexpectedly and wonderfully, they gave me the gig, which completely changed my life.

It's odd isn't it, two future Goodies auditioning a future Python? All from Pembroke. But what joy for me as at the start of the next term I joined Jonathan Lynn, and Tim and Bill, in the Pembroke College Smoking Concert on a tiny stage in a corner of a packed Old Reader for three nights of hilarity. Imagine a not-particularly-large room, an ex-nineteenth-century library, with gabled windows and leaded glass, packed with tables and candles, undergraduates and their dates dressed to the nines, a lot of wine and a great deal of smoke. A small, raised, brightly lit platform in one corner was the stage and on it performed the cast, led by Tim and Bill. There was one very funny girl (Carol), Lynn, a pianist and one fresh-faced young newcomer: me. One of the sketches I did was an Old Testament Newsreader played by Bill, called BBC BC.

> News from Mount Ararat where Moses is negotiating a Commandment deal with God Almighty. A spokesman for Moses says he's tough, but the good news is they've cut him down to Ten. The bad news is Adultery is still in.

I then played the Biblical Weather Forecaster, to huge laughs.

> Good Even. Well let's take a quick look at the scroll. We've a plague of locusts moving in from the North West, scattered outbreaks of fire and brimstone in Tarsus and some mild thunderbolts, force two to three, here in Gath...

I didn't know it at the time, but that part was written by John Cleese for himself. I had no idea who he was, or that, at 23, he was a senior member of the Footlights, for I was just a 19-year-old freshman at Cambridge and didn't know that the only reason that John wasn't on stage himself was that, though he wined and dined in Pembroke nightly and everyone assumed he was at Pembroke, he wasn't actually a member of the College. He was at Downing. So I played his part and amazingly he was there, watching my first ever public performance. Afterwards, in the euphoria, a very tall man in a thick tweed suit with dark hair and piercing dark eyes was introduced to me by Humphrey Barclay. How odd of the Comedy Gods to have arranged two future Pythons and two future Goodies all in the same room in February 1963. Remember this is even pre-Beatles. They are still getting hammered in Hamburg and we have never heard of them. But John was very kind

Eric Idle (right) with Humphrey Barclay.

and complimentary, and indeed encouraging, urging me to go along and audition for the Footlights at their next Smoker.

Of course I had never heard of the Footlights either, but I soon discovered it was The University Revue Club founded in 1883. It seemed like a fun thing to do and a month later Jonathan Lynn and I were voted in by the Committee, after having faced the ordeal of performing live to a packed crowd of comedy buffs on the slightly more glamorous Footlights stage, in the private Footlights Club in Neals' Yard, above fishy-smelling Mac Fisheries. I remember the sketch played surprisingly well. So right there my life changed. I never got a proper job again in my life. By March, thanks to Tim, I had been elected to the Footlights, where Tim was President. Graeme Garden would be President the next year, and I was President the year after. A Pembroke sandwich.

That summer the Footlights Annual Revue, which ran for two weeks during May Week at the Cambridge Arts Theatre, was the funniest thing I had seen since *Beyond The Fringe*. It was a particularly funny year and the Cambridge Footlights Revue, after five months on stage in the West End, actually ended up on Broadway. And with it a sketch I wrote – a parody of the Beatles doing the Hallelujah chorus. A precursor to The Rutles.

I soon adapted to Footlights Club life. We had our own private bar which opened at 10 at night and stayed open as long as we wanted. (Pubs closed at 10.30.) Lunches were provided inexpensively on the premises and twice a term there were Smoking Concerts where one could try out new material. So much about comedy is confidence. That was the most valuable thing about the Footlights: learning the art of being a writer/performer by watching and doing. Learning how to write, rewrite and cut sketch material, I still had to go out and learn performing in front of quite difficult audiences.

In my short time there I experienced almost every kind of audience. We performed cabaret professionally at least twice a week. We played in theatres, we played at Edinburgh Festivals,

Eric Idle at the launch of the Mill Lane fundraising campaign, 'The Time and the Place', in March 2017.

Eric Idle at the campaign launch in March 2017, with some of the Pembroke Choir.

before factory audiences, before dinner-jacketed hoorays and ball-gowned debs, in Butlin's holiday camps, before drunks, before dinner, before Round Table businessmen and ultimately in radio and television studios. Had one sat down to plan a crash course in showbusiness, one could hardly have bettered this as a learning experience. A University which permits such activity is clearly doing its job, by doing absolutely nothing. Despite complaints about the Footlights – that it is somehow too professional (but then who wants amateur comedy?), that it is elitist (though nobody laughs because they are impressed by the social rank of those on stage),

that it is privileged (nobody laughs out of kindness either) and that it is undergraduate (they *are*, after all, undergraduates) – it has nevertheless self-created its own tradition. A tradition which seeks after excellence, and then seeks to hide that excellence.

Ars est celare artem.

So I am proud to be an Honorary Fellow of Pembroke College. I am proud that Pembroke is expanding, pushing on down to the river. With Professor Brian Cox we are hoping that they will name something 'The Idle Cox Boathouse...'.

16 Pembroke Today: The Buildings We Made Our Own

Gwenno Robinson

'Don't become friends with the first people you meet' is the advice doled out like clockwork to Freshers each year. 'Finding "your people" takes time,' I was warned a dozen times or more in the weeks and days before I first moved to Cambridge.

As it turned out I didn't have to wait very long nor venture very far.

My first night at Pembroke was a dark, rainy evening. Although it was only a few days into October, it felt as if we were already in the depths of winter. Unsure what else to do, I embarked on a treasure hunt organised by the College. I trailed behind a large group of strangers, not knowing where to turn or who to speak to.

On our way to finding the first clue, we reached the top floor of Foundress Court, the big, modern building into which I, and a hundred other first-years, had just moved. On the opposite end of the corridor was a dimly lit kitchen, filled with people whose laughter echoed through the building.

Gwenno Robinson lived in Room AA39 in Foundress Court during her first year at Pembroke College.

I couldn't turn away. I took a deep breath and stumbled into a Foundress kitchen for the first time. It was there I found a group of people huddled around a pack of cards, like cavemen gathered around a fire, nestling in closer for warmth.

The air was thick with humidity and the rain battered against the glass windows, using all its might to join us too. I pulled up a chair and

The view from Bowling Green Lawn towards Foundress Court, where Gwenno Robinson lived in her first year. Henry Moore's Figure in a Shelter *stands in front of the new buildings.*

abandoned the treasure hunt. I had found what I was looking for. These were 'my people' and I knew I had struck gold. It was in these kitchens that we cooked elaborate meals on the George Forman grill and the two hobs we had. Although we didn't have an oven, it didn't hold back our culinary horizons. We soon learned that the fire alarms were sensitive: setting them off triggered a £100 fine and a public telling off from the porters. I'm still not sure which I'd rather face.

In my first year I was the only girl in a household of seven boys. I befriended two of them almost instantly, partly out of concern for their welfare and my own.

One of the people I found in the kitchen that first night was Max, who turned out to be my next-door neighbour in Foundress. Only a day between us in age, we soon became the closest of friends. A year later he got down on one knee and became my (College) husband.

The other, Jude, lived on the furthest end of the corridor and studied Politics like me. I used to thump on his door in the mornings to wake him in time for our lectures. Every morning we just about ran to Sidgwick, clutching pieces of burnt toast. As much as we tried to be on time, we never were.

We were very thankful to be attending lectures in person as the remnants of the Covid-19 pandemic loomed over us. We knew how lucky we were, only narrowly escaping the misfortune of having lockdowns, masks and social distancing spill into our university experience.

We roamed freely down the long corridors of Foundress Court, meeting people from all floors of the building. Stripes of black-and-yellow security tape, marking out the old households that had existed during Covid, served as a daily reminder of how different our reality could have been.

In February of my first year we got a taste of what life could have been like when a wave of

The entrance to AA Staircase in Foundress Court, built by Eric Parry in 1997.

Covid spread around the College like wildfire. Before long we were all in isolation, waiting for the two lines on our tests to change to one. I remember going to the Master's Garden to play a round of catch, assembling with my friends, eager for some fresh air. We were a sorry sight, in blue sterile masks and baggy pyjamas.

In my second year I lived in 26 Barton Road. My group of friends and I stumbled upon it when trying to choose a house at the end of our first year. We soon learned that we were the only group to make the trek to visit the house, which was in a quiet part of Newnham, around the back of Sidgwick.

When we saw it for the first time, we all gasped. It was a grand old house, boasting seven large bedrooms, a garden, a greenhouse and an empty annex. It had tall, sandstone columns which held up the regal-looking porch. Each room had high ceilings, giving way to huge bay windows which glistened in the morning sun. It certainly was not a house intended for students and we couldn't believe our luck. It fitted our group of seven friends like a glove, feeling as if it had been made for us.

One of the main attractions of the house was its location. A 20-minute walk from the College, situated out of the watchful eyes of the porters, it seemed like the perfect location to make up for the years of our youth that we'd lost to the pandemic. Even more so when we discovered that our neighbour – an elderly man in his nineties – was partially deaf. We paid him a visit and tentatively asked how he would feel about us having a party or two.

'Don't you worry about me, I can't hear a thing,' he reassured us.

We took that as our blessing and hosted a party for every birthday or celebration we could think of, or sometimes just because we could. My fondest memories of university are set in our Barton Road kitchen, the windows wide open, music blasting and a hundred or so students from all Colleges spilling out of the house and into the garden.

The only slight problem was that the kitchen and corridors were all fitted with a stark automatic light – I imagine to deter such gatherings from

The interior of Pembroke's Dining Hall, built by Waterhouse in 1875 and extended in 1925. Students gather here regularly to dine together in what are universally known as 'formals'.

happening in the first place. But we took it in our stride, sticking tea towels and orange plastic bags to block the light as much as we could. Most of my memories of our parties are tainted with the distinctive orange glow of Sainsbury's bags, pressed up against the white lights.

After spending a year living in College, having our own garden was a novelty. After sleepless May Ball nights we spent long summer days barely lifting sore heads from the grass outside. Our kitchen table remained outside for the best part of June.

My friends and I were the final group of students to live in the house. On our final day there kitchen appliances were ripped out of the wall as renovations began to turn the house into a children's nursery for Pembroke and Queens'. Although the building itself is no longer as we remember it, I hold 26 Barton Road and the

Above left *The community kitchens for students living in Dolby Court are large, well equipped and all electric. They are a major improvement on the facilities in the historic College.*

Left *The rear of the Dining Hall, looking from Red Buildings.*

Above *A bust of Lord Chief Justice Taylor, made by Michael Rizzello. It presides over the Law Library that is named after him.*

memories we made in it very close to my heart. So much so, my group of friends and I have referred to our group as 'The Barton Lot' ever since.

However, many of my fondest memories don't take place in the houses where I stayed, but within the four walls of Pembroke College and its gardens. It was in Pembroke Café, clutching cups of hot coffee, that we put the world in its place – usually with tears of laughter, joy or exhaustion, often all three, streaming down our faces. As much as we tried to convince ourselves that we were working, hours would go by and the word count of our essays would remain unchanged.

We spent long-winded brunches at 'Trough' (Pembroke's Servery), speaking in hushed tones as we debriefed each other about the antics of the night before. We'd remain in the dining hall until we were the only ones left and the catering staff were laying the plates for dinner.

I realise at this point that I should probably mention some libraries to avoid giving the wrong impression of my university days. Each year we found a different fondness for a different part of the Library. In the first year I remember spending long Sundays in the Law Library, where more talking was done than reading.

Revising for exams in summer felt like torture, especially as we could see the gardens bloom before our very eyes. In the run up to our final exams, my friends and I studied in the Art Library. The room had big arching windows which let in the warm sun; it was the closest we could get to being outside.

We'd sometimes attempt to work outside, but never successfully. Long afternoons were spent lying back on the grass of the Bowling Green, eyes shut, moving only to catch the sun's rays. If anyone so much as flinched to get back up to the Library, you'd almost certainly hear a groan of 'Five more minutes…'.

I read somewhere that there's nothing quite as sad as realising in the moment just how much you're going to miss it. It's how I can best describe my entire time at university, but the feeling was especially heightened in our final weeks at Pembroke, as the final term drew to a close. One part of us eager to get out and see the world for all its worth; but another part of us hanging on to what we had left, with no intention of letting it go.

I vividly remember dawn breaking at the end of the Pembroke May Ball in our final year. As the sun rose that day, it felt as if it was ushering in a new age and setting on another. And in many ways it was.

We sang Robbie Williams's *Angels*, just as we had at every May Ball before, our voices cracking, heavy with emotion. We could barely look at each other, knowing the tears it would trigger. We held onto each other and those final moments of blissful, youthful ignorance we knew we'd miss so much.

Behind us, centuries-old buildings looked on, the same buildings that towered over us as naive 18-year-olds, their outline forever etched into recollections of our time at Pembroke. They are the walls we covered in fairy lights and photographs, beaming as we laughed and wincing as we cried.

They've seen it all: the joy, the grief, the love and the heartbreak, witnessing all the things we got wrong and everything we did right. They know what we got up to better than our parents or the porters ever did – or ever will.

These are the buildings that we made our own. Our presence in them fleeting, and over in the blink of an eye.

The Art Library, gifted to the College by publisher and critic Tom Rosenthal, is a favourite place for students of all subjects to study.

16 PEMBROKE TODAY: THE BUILDINGS WE MADE OUR OWN

Timeline

Alternative dates linked to a person or event have been highlighted in **bold**

1347 Letters patent sealed at Guildford by King Edward III granting Marie de St Pol the right to found a house of 30 scholars in the town of Cambridge.

1346–63 Three plots of land acquired by the Foundress for the College site. Plot 1 (**1346**) was what is now the site of the Old Library.

1355 Pope Innocent VI grants permission for the building of a Chapel.

1369 Marie de St Pol conveys a farm at Burwell that she had purchased in **1349** to trustees who held it for the College.

1377 Death of Marie de St Pol.

*c.***1385** First College Chapel (now the Old Library) completed.

*c.***1389** Old Court (in its original smaller, blocked-off incarnation) completed.

1440 Benefactions of King Edward VI: Linton Priory with the chapel at Isleham and the manor and advowson of Soham, all in Cambridgeshire.

1450 Laurence Booth elected Master.

1452 Library built above the Dining Hall.

*c.***1470** The Foundress Cup probably given by Richard Sockborn, admitted Fellow of the College *c.***1470** and Vicar of Soham.

1497 The Anathema Cup given by Thomas Langton, admitted Fellow of the College **1461** and later Provost of The Queen's College, Oxford.

1507–8 Lectureship in Theology founded at Pembroke by Sir John Hussey, Comptroller of the Royal Household.

1526 William Turner admitted to Pembroke. Elected Fellow of Pembroke *c.***1530–1**. Turner's *Herbal* published in three parts **1551–68**.

1540 Nicholas Ridley elected Master. Admitted to College *c.***1518**. Admitted Fellow in **1524**. Martyred in **1555**.

1569 Edmund Spenser matriculates at Pembroke. *The Shepheardes Calender* published in **1579**. *The Faerie Queene* published in **1590**.

1576 Edmund Grindall made Archbishop of Canterbury.

1589 Lancelot Andrewes elected Master; goes on to lead the creation of the King James Bible.

1598 William Smart donates manuscripts originally from the Abbey at Bury St Edmunds.

1601 Matthew Wren admitted to Pembroke. Wren awarded his BA and admitted Fellow of the College in **1604/5**. Elected President of Pembroke in **1616** and Master of Peterhouse in **1625**. Died and buried in the vault of the new College Chapel in **1667**.

*c.***1614** Work begins on the north side (Pembroke Street) of what is now known as Ivy Court.

1636 Roger Williams (a Pembroke alumnus) founds settlement at Providence, Rhode Island; he is regarded as the founder of the state of Rhode Island.

1636 Sir Robert Hitcham's bequest of Framlingham Castle in Suffolk, along with associated lands.

1643 Dowsing purges the Chapel of 'superstitious imagery'.

1658 Nehemiah Grew admitted to Pembroke. *The Anatomy of Plants* by Grew published in **1682**

1659–61 Hitcham Building (south range of what is now Ivy Court) built.

1662 Mark Franck elected Master. Died in **1664**, leaving a large collection of books to the College.

1662 Christopher Wren invited to design a new College Chapel.

1665 New Chapel (the gift of Matthew Wren) consecrated.

1675 Thomas Thanet rebuilds the organ in the new Chapel.

*c.***1690** Work to transform the Old Chapel into a Library completed.

1697 Roger Long admitted to Pembroke. Elected to a Fellowship in **1703**. Elected Master in **1733**.

1708 Chapel organ replaced and old organ transferred to Framlingham Church, where it can still be seen today. Within Pembroke's Chapel a new organ installed, built by Charles Quarles.

From 1712 Walls of Old Court faced with Ketton stone (a Jurassic oolitic limestone).

1739 Christopher Smart matriculates at Pembroke. Admitted Fellow in **1745**.

1743 College celebrates 400th anniversary, having previously considered its foundation date to be **1443**.

1756/7 Thomas Gray migrates to Pembroke from Peterhouse. Appointed Regius Professor of History and Modern Languages in **1768**.

1773 William Pitt admitted to Pembroke at the age of 14.

1807 Sara Lonsdale bequest.

1827 Pembroke College Boat Club formed.

1828 Gilbert Ainslie elected Master.

1833 College adds Paschal Close to its site, on which now stand the Pitt Buildings, Old Master's Lodge and New Court.

1847 College celebrates its 500th anniversary.

1853 John Couch Adams, mathematician and astronomer who predicted the existence and position of Neptune, joins Pembroke as a Fellow.

1861 College purchases land from Peterhouse on which Foundress Court now stands.

1862 Pembroke College Debating Society founded.

By 1862 Renovation of the Dining Hall by John Cory completed.

1869 College Statutes changed to allow Fellows to be married.

1871 The Sphere (the first-ever planetarium) created by Roger Long (Master, 1733–70) dismantled.

1872 Red Buildings designed by Alfred Waterhouse completed.

1873 New Master's Lodge by Waterhouse completed.

1874–5 Old Master's Lodge demolished with the removal of the south range of Old Court, thereby opening up the view of the Chapel from the College entrance.

1875–6 New Hall designed by Waterhouse built.

1878 New Library designed by Waterhouse completed.

1881 Consecration of extension of Chapel. The extension was designed by G.G. Scott Jr.

1881–2 New Court built by G.G. Scott Jr.

1885 College Mission (now Pembroke House in Walworth) held its first general meeting. Mission inaugurated in **1886**.

1902 E.G. Browne becomes Sir Thomas Adams's Professor of Arabic.

1903 George Gabriel Stokes elected Master. **1837** Admitted to College as a pensioner in 1837, then became Fellow, **1841–57** and **1869–1902**. He was Lucasian Professor **1849–1903** and served as MP for the University **1887–91**.

1906 Stained glass installed in the East window of the Chapel. The windows were designed and executed by Godfrey Wood Humphry.

1907 Pitt Building (M Staircase) completed, designed by W.D. Caröe. He also designed O Staircase and the bridge joining the Pitt Building to New Court.

1910 Harry Frank Guggenheim admitted to Pembroke, gaining his BA in **1913**. H.F. Guggenheim's first benefaction to Pembroke made **1929**.

1913 Arthur Bliss takes his BA and Mus.B. He became Master of the Queen's Music in **1953**.

1920 Pembroke College Cambridge Society founded.

1924 First World War memorial by T.H. Lyons unveiled and dedicated.

1925–6 The flat ceiling returns to the Dining Hall and two storeys are added above by Maurice Webb. The wall between the Hall and the Fellows' combination room is also removed, creating a high table dais.

1929 College purchases Denny Abbey, burial place of Marie de St Pol.

1929–32 Robert 'Robin' Orr is organ scholar at the College; made Honorary Fellow in **1989**.

1931 Gandhi visits Pembroke.

1933 New Master's Lodge facing Tennis Court Road built by Maurice Webb.

1936 Meredith Dewey joins Pembroke College as Dean after completing a cycle ride from Ostend to Jerusalem.

1937 Sir Montagu Butler elected Master.

1941 R.A. Butler (later Deputy Prime Minister) elected Honorary Fellow, having been an undergraduate at the College.

1947 A.J. Arberry appointed Sir Thomas Adams's Professor of Arabic.

1949 Hall windows replaced by Murray Easton.

1950 Kamau Brathwaite, Caribbean writer and poet, matriculates at Pembroke. Made an Honorary Fellow in **2018**.

1951 Ted Hughes matriculates at Pembroke after completing his national service.

1951 A.J.B. Wace elected Honorary Fellow, having been an undergraduate at the College.

1955 Pembroke Players formed.

1957 Orchard Building completed to the design of Marshall Sisson.

1957 Queen Elizabeth, The Queen Mother, visits Pembroke.

1957 Ray Dolby joins the College as a Marshall Scholar to work on his PhD. He was elected to the Fellowship in **1960** as the then Drapers' Senior Research Student, then became the Drapers' Research Fellow after receiving his PhD in **1961**.

1960 A.J. Arberry sets up Cambridge Centre of Middle Eastern Studies.

1962 Erwin Rosenthal, scholar, bookseller and art historian, admitted Fellow of the College.

1972 Rodney Robert Porter (Pembroke 1946) and Gerald Edelman share the Nobel Prize for Physiology or Medicine for resolving the structure and mode of action of antibodies.

1977 First students from the University of California attend short programmes at Pembroke over the long vacation – the forerunner of today's international programmes.

1980 Rebuilding of the College organ by Mander.

1983 Vote for co-residency passed by the College Meeting. Valerie Kyle, the first female Fellow, elected; female graduate students admitted.

1983 William Fowler (Pembroke 1955) and Subrahmanyan Chandrasekhar win the Nobel Prize in Physics for the evolution and devolution of stars.

1984 Female undergraduate students admitted to the College.

1985 Malcolm Lyons appointed Sir Thomas Adams's Professor of Arabic, the third Pembroke holder.

1992 Jo Cox (née Leadbeater) joins Pembroke as an undergraduate.

1996 Master's Lodge demolished to make way for Foundress Court.

1996 The Pembroke Corporate Partnership Programme established.

1996 William Pitt Fellowships introduced.

1997 Completion of Foundress Court and the New Master's Lodge, designed by Eric Parry.

2001 Simon Gibson Wing of the Library opens for student use. It expands Library and Archive storage space and includes the new Peter Taylor Law Library – named in honour of the late Lord Taylor of Gosforth (Pembroke 1950), Lord Chief Justice of England 1992–6.

2002 John Sulston (Pembroke 1960) wins the Nobel Prize in Physiology or Medicine for his work on the cell lineage and genome of the worm Caenorhabditis elegans, alongwith his colleagues Sydney Brenner and Robert Horvitz at the MRC Laboratory of Molecular Biology.

2016 Anna Lapwood joins Pembroke as the College's first female Director of Music.

2019 Inaugural Pembroke Environment Seminar.

2022 Leadership, Enterprise and Adventure at Pembroke: the LEAP Programme launched.

SOURCES

Pembroke College Archives

Pembroke College Society Annual Gazettes

Pembroke Portraits, A.V. Grimston (2013)

Building Pembroke Chapel: Wren, Pearce and Scott, A.V. Grimston (2009).

Pembroke College: A Celebration, A.V. Grimstone (ed.) (1997).

A Short History of Pembroke College Cambridge, Aubrey Attwater, edited by S.C. Roberts (1973).

Acknowledgements

My first thanks are to all the Fellows of Pembroke, for encouraging me in the endeavour that has culminated in this wonderful tribute to our College. I then approached a range of potential writers of chapters, including some alumni, some Fellows, some of those directly engaged in the development of the Mill Lane site, and a recently graduated student. They all readily agreed, and the result is a series of insightful contributions that make up the text of the book. Will Pryce stepped up to take most of the photographs, spending many days in the College and responding to innumerable requests for specific images. Other photographers have also helpfully contributed. My grateful thanks to all of them, and especially to Will. The editors and designers from Scala – Catherine Bradley, Claire Young, and Matt Wilson from Mexington – could not have been more helpful. A big thank you to them. Photographic and copyright credits are noted elsewhere. Any errors and omissions are entirely down to me.

Chris Smith

CONTRIBUTORS

Lord Chris Smith of Finsbury, Master of Pembroke College, Cambridge

Beatie Blakemore, Haworth Tompkins, Architects

Polly Blakesley, Fellow in Art History, Pembroke College

Chris Blencowe, former Bursar, Pembroke College

Andrew Cates, Bursar, Pembroke College

Sarah Claydon, Head Gardener, Pembroke College

Kurosh Davis, Tom Stuart-Smith, Landscape Architects

Dagmar Dolby, President of the Ray and Dagmar Dolby Family Fund

Elizabeth Ennion-Smith, Archivist, Pembroke College

Stephen Gage, alumnus and architectural historian

James Gardom, Dean and Chaplain, Pembroke College

Loraine Gelsthorpe, Chair of the Fellows' Gardens Committee

Joel Gustafsson, JG Consulting, Environmental Engineers

Stephen Halliday, alumnus and Cambridge guide

Eric Idle, alumnus, actor and writer

Mark Purcell, Bye-Fellow and Deputy Director of Cambridge University Library

Gwenno Robinson, Pembroke student 2021–4 and Orwell Prize Winner

Mark Wormald, Fellow in English, Pembroke College

PHOTOGRAPHIC CREDITS

Endpapers, pp. 12–13, 50, 100: Ian Fleming; front and back covers, frontispiece, pp. 8–10, 20–3, 25–9, 31, 37, 39, 41, 44, 46 (left), 48–9, 51, 55, 57, 62, 63, 65, 66 (top and bottom), 67 (top two), 76–7, 79, 80–1, 82, 84–5, 86 (bottom), 87, 88–90, 91 (top), 92–3, 94–5, 96–7, 99, 101–5, 106–7, 108–12, 114–15, 117–30, 131 (top), 133, 134, 135–7, 139–40, 150–3, 154 (top right and bottom), 155: Will Pryce; p. 6 and back flap: Barbara Luckhurst; p. 7: Igor Sterner; p. 11: Iona Warne; pp. 14, 98: National Portrait Gallery; pp. 15, 16, 19, 88, 91 (bottom), 131 (bottom); 145 (right): Archives of Pembroke College; p. 17: Fitzwilliam Museum; pp. 18, 38, 40, 41 (right), 52, 64, 67 (bottom), 70 (right) 71–3, 84–5, 86 (top), 134 (top), 154 (top): Sally March; p. 24: James Anderson; pp. 32, 43, 70 (left): Haworth Tompkins; pp. 33, 35, 43, 73 (top), 74: Fred Howarth; pp. 34, 38, 60, 70 (right), 71, 72, 73 (bottom): David Valinksy; p. 42: Cambridge City Council (Old Press/Mill Lane Supplementary Planning Document); p. 47: Allies & Morrison; p. 53: Dolby Family Archive; p. 54: By kind permission of the archives of Cambridge Assessment; pp. 56, 58: Historic England; p. 60: David Valinsky; p. 61: Tom Stuart-Smith; p. 69: Joel Gustafsson; pp. 104–5 (bottom): Alice Oates; p. 113: Albi Rix; p. 114: Will Pryce; p. 132: Keith Heppell; p. 134 (bottom): Stephen White & Co; pp. 145 (left), 145 (top): Eric Idle; pp. 148–9: Nigel Luckhurst.

COPYRIGHT CREDITS

All images are © Archives of Pembroke College, Cambridge, unless stated below: p. 6: © The History of Parliament Trust; p. 11: Extract from 'Ash Wednesday' from *Collected Poems 1909–1962* by T.S. Eliot © Set Copyrights Limited. Reused by permission of Faber and Faber Ltd; p. 14: © National Portrait Gallery; p. 17: © Syndics of the Fitzwilliam Museum; p. 23, 136–7, 143: © The artist; p. 32: © Haworth Tompkins; pp. 37, 48–9, 65, 74, 124–5, 129, 131 (top): © The artist; p. 41: © The artist; p. 54: © by kind permission of the Assessment Archives of Cambridge University Press and Assessment; p. 56: © Historic England; pp. 80–1, 135: © The artist; p. 91 (bottom): © Archives of Pembroke College; p. 98: © National Portrait Gallery; p. 126: © Tom Phillips. All Rights Reserved, DACS 2024; p. 127: © The artist; p. 128 (both): © The artist; p. 130: © The artist; p. 132: © The artist; pp. 133, 151: © The Henry Moore Foundation; p. 134 (top): © The artist; p. 134 © The artist; p. 139: © Estate of Ted Hughes; reproduced by permission of Faber and Faber Ltd; p. 140: © The artist; p. 154: © The artist.

Pembroke College and Scala Arts & Heritage are committed to respecting the intellectual property rights of others. We have taken all reasonable efforts to ensure that the reproduction of all contents on these pages is done with the full consent of the copyright owners. If you are aware of unintentional omissions, please contact the company directly so that any necessary corrections may be made for future editions.